A. KIRK GRAYSON is a professor in the Department of Near Eastern Studies at the University of Toronto. He studied Assyriology at the University of Vienna under Professor W. von Soden, and received his Ph.D. in Assyriology from The Johns Hopkins University. His thesis, written under the supervision of Professor W. G. Lambert, was on ancient Mesopotamian chronological texts; Assyro-Babylonian historiography has continued to be the main area of his research. He has traveled extensively in North America, Europe, and the Near East in search of cuneiform inscriptions, and has published numerous articles and two books: *Assyrian and Babylonian Chronicles* and *Assyrian Royal Inscriptions*.

DONALD B. REDFORD is a professor in the Department of Near Eastern Studies at the University of Toronto. Educated at the University of Toronto and Brown University, he is author of several books and articles on Egypt and the Near East, including *History and Chronology of the Egyptian Eighteenth Dynasty, Seven Studies* and *A Study of the Biblical Joseph Story*. He has participated as site supervisor and epigrapher in excavations at Jerusalem and at Buto in Lower Egypt, and since 1970 has directed an archaeological expedition to Karnak in Upper Egypt. In 1972 he also became director of the Akhenaten Temple Project of the University Museum, University of Pennsylvania.

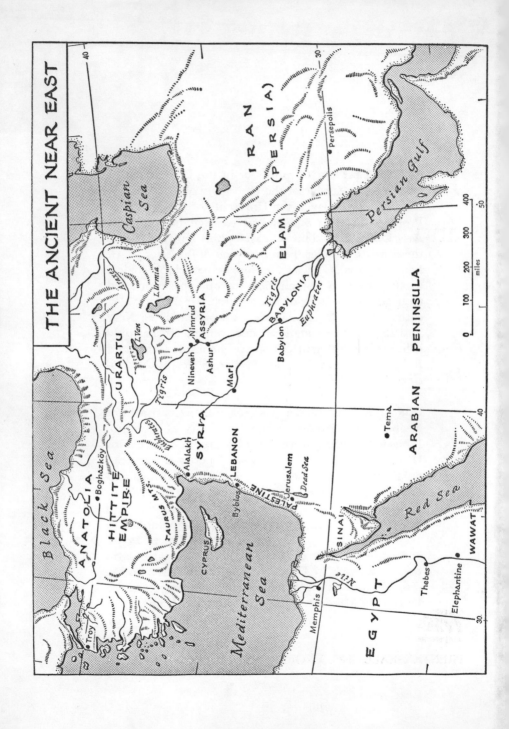

THE ANCIENT NEAR EAST

PAPYRUS
and TABLET

edited by

A. Kirk Grayson
Donald B. Redford

A SPECTRUM BOOK

PRENTICE-HALL, INC. ENGLEWOOD CLIFFS, N.J.

Library of Congress Cataloging in Publication Data

GRAYSON, ALBERT KIRK, comp.
   Papyrus and tablet.

   (A Spectrum Book)
   Bibliography: p.
   1. Egyptian literature—Translations into English.
2. English literature—Translations from Egyptian.
I. Redford, Donald B., joint comp.   II. Title.
PJ1943.G7   893'.1   73–7734
ISBN 0–13–648394–1
ISBN 0–13–648386–0 (pbk.)

10   9   8   7   6   5   4   3   2   1

PRENTICE-HALL INTERNATIONAL, INC. (*London*)
PRENTICE-HALL OF AUSTRALIA PTY. LTD. (*Sydney*)
PRENTICE-HALL OF CANADA, LTD. (*Toronto*)
PRENTICE-HALL OF INDIA PRIVATE LIMITED (*New Delhi*)
PRENTICE-HALL OF JAPAN, INC. (*Tokyo*)

PREFACE

The ancient Near East is usually understood as encompassing the lands between the Caucasus on the north, Ethiopia on the south, the Aegean on the west, and the highlands of eastern Iran on the east. For the historian the foci of attention in this area are the Nile valley, and the broad plains enclosed by the Tigris and Euphrates, called by the Greeks Mesopotamia, "the land between the rivers." Here, in the Fourth Millennium B.C., the earliest thoroughgoing urban cultures in the world took form, organized upon a dependency on artificial irrigation which has to one historian, at least, justified the appellative "hydraulic."

Today this region supports a welter of peoples and cultures, but in antiquity the heterogeneous nature of the component states was even more marked. Where now Arabic and Islam predominate, four millennia ago a number of now defunct dialects and religions vied with one another. Through most of the three thousand years cov-

v

ered by this book the great family of Semitic languages stands out as dominant linguistically. On the east it was represented by Akkadian, the language of Akkad, spoken originally by the inhabitants of the Babylonian plain in the latitude of modern Baghdad, but later widely used as a diplomatic and literary dialect. In the lands bordering the Mediterranean were a group of closely related "West-Semitic" languages, of which Hebrew is the best known, but which also included Amorite, Phoenician and Aramaic. Around the edge of the great crescent formed by the geographical distribution of these dialects were strewn, mainly in the highlands of Anatolia, Armenia and Iran, older language groups whose affinities are unknown to us. One may mention Luwian in Anatolia, Subarian in Armenia, Hurrian in northern Mesopotamia, Elamite in Elam, and Sumerian in southern Iraq. By the middle of the Second Millennium B.C. the ingressing Hittites in Anatolia were writing their language in Babylonian cuneiform, thus becoming the first Indo-European speaking people to commit their tongue to writing. Finally, on the south beyond the land bridge to Africa, flourished the ancient Egyptian language, a curiously isolated phenomenon showing remote connexions with Semitic and African tongues.

As all knowledge of these languages, their scripts and the peoples who spoke them had been long lost before the beginning of the European Middle Ages, the entire Ancient History of the Near East has had to be painstakingly recovered by an inductive approach, using almost exclusively the results of archaeology. For the past century and a half Egypt, Mesopotamia, Syria and Palestine have been subjected to an increasingly intensive programme of exploration and excavation. But artifacts and architecture can tell us only a little about the spiritual accomplishments of a people; by far the major portion of the evidence must come from written documents. Where a literature exists there is true civilization.

Little of the vast literatures of ancient Mesopotamia and Egypt is available in translation to the modern reader. What selections have appeared in the past few decades are primarily designed for students of the Bible and are not representative of the scope and nature of the native material. In the narrow confines of this small book we also have not been able to provide a representative sampling of the various kinds of written documents from the two ancient civilizations. Rather we have each selected six topics and presented documents in translation to illustrate these. The topics were chosen either because they are an outstanding feature of the ancient culture or because they are particularly relevant in our modern world. Obviously neither the themes presented nor the documents translated are a comprehensive collection. But it is our hope that this slim volume will tempt many readers to pass on to more substantial readings for which purpose a bibliography is included.

The conceptual barriers between ancient and modern man and between eastern and western man are a constant source of misunderstanding and misinterpretation. There is no simple means of overcoming these obstacles. However we have attempted to minimize their effect by illustrating the selected themes as much as possible with translations of original documents and, further, by presenting rather free translations unencumbered by scholarly apparatus (square brackets, footnotes, etc.). Our main concern is that the reader may savour the repast that awaits him in the ancient words inscribed on papyrus and tablet.

CONTENTS

To

W. Stewart McCullough
Teacher, Colleague, Friend

CHRONOLOGICAL CHART

Date	Egypt	Babylonia	Assyria
3300		"Protoliterate Period"	
3200	Union of Egypt under Menes (c. 3050)		
3100			
3000	"Protodynastic Period" (Dynasties 1–2)	Invention of writing	
2900			
2800	Invention of writing		
2700	Development of Calendar	"Early Dynastic Period"	
2600			
2500	"Old Kingdom"		
2400	Pyramid Age (Dynasties 3–6)		
2300		"Old Akkadian Period" Sargon (c. 2334–2279) Naram-Sin (c. 2254–2218)	
2200		Guti	
2100	"First Intermediate" (Dynasties 7–10)	"Ur III Period" Amorites	
2000	"Middle Kingdom" (Dynasties 11–13)	"Early Old Babylonian Period"	Amorites
1900		Isin-Larsa rivalry	
1800	Colonization of Nubia	"Old Babylonian Period"	Shamshi-Adad I (c. 1813–1781)
1700		Hammurapi (c. 1792–1750)	Zimri-lim of Mari
1600	Hyksos Domination (Dynasty 15)	Hittite sack of Babylon (c. 1595)	
1500	"New Kingdom" (Dynasties 17–20) Empire in the Sudan & Syria	"Dark Ages" Kassite Dynasty	Vassal of Mitanni
1400			
1300	Egypto-Hittite war (c. 1350–1270)	Kassite-Egyptian correspondence	Ashur-uballit I (c. 1365–1330)
1200	Invasion of Sea Peoples	Vassal of Assyria	"Middle Assyrian Empire" Tukulti-Ninurta I (c. 1244–1208)
1100		Fall of Kassites (c. 1157)	
1000	"Tanite Kingdom" (Dynasty 21) Economic decline, loss of empire	Nebuchadnezzar I (c. 1126–1105) Intensive literary activity	
900	"Libyan Period" (Dynasties 22–24)	Aramaeans	"Kalach Period" Ashurnasirapli II (883–859) Shalmaneser III (858–824)
800		Vassal of Assyria	Shamshi-Adad V (823–811) Adad-nerari III (810–783) Tiglath-pileser III (744–727)
700	Sabeco conquers Egypt "Kushite-Saite Period" (Dynasties 25–26)	Merodach-baladan	Sargon II (721–705) Sennacherib (704–681) Esarhaddon (680–669) Ashurbanipal (668–627)
600		"Neo-Babylonian Empire" Nebuchadnezzar II (604–562)	Fall of Nineveh (612)
500	Fall of Egypt (525)	Nabonidus (555–539)	Vassal of Babylonia
400		Fall of Babylon (539)	
300		PERSIAN EMPIRE	

Iran	Syro-Palestine	Anatolia	Date
			3300
			3200
	Early Bronze I		3100
			3000
			2900
Proto-Elamite Writing	Early Bronze II		2800
			2700
Elam			2600
	Early Bronze III		2500
			2400
			2300
	Early Bronze IV		2200
	Amorite Invasion		2100
			2000
	Amorite States	Old Assyrian Merchant Colony	1900
			1800
		Old Hittite Kingdom	1700
			1600
	Kingdom of Mitanni		1500
		New Hittite Kingdom Suppiluliumas (c. 1375–1330)	1400
	Mitanni destroyed alphabet	Battle of Kadesh (c. 1285)	1300
		Fall of Hittites & Troy Phrygians (Mushki)	1200
Indo-Aryans	Aramaeans, Hebrews, Neo-Hittites, Philistines		1100
			1000
Assyrian Invasion	Hebrew Monarchy Assyrian Invasion	Assyrian Invasion	900
Urartu Medes, Persians, Scythians	Urartu Assyrian Campaigns Fall of Samaria (721)	Assyrian Campaigns	800
Urartu destroyed Elam destroyed		Gyges	700
			600
Median Empire Achaemenid Dynasty Cyrus II (559–530)	Fall of Jerusalem (587) Exile	Fall of Sardis (546)	500
			400
PERSIAN EMPIRE			300

1

"The King of Upper and Lower Egypt"

The Egyptian State

One of the most appealing characteristics of the ancient Egyptians was their willingness to cooperate to make their society work. Indeed, in a country where the very life of the people depended on working together to harness the power of the yearly inundation, a man had to cooperate with his neighbour, or starve. With a season of laxity, or a year of internal strife, the irrigation system would fall into ruin, and famine become a real possibility. Labour thus had to be organized to produce and distribute food as quickly an as efficiently as possible. This required a strong central government, with a strong man at its head. Small wonder, then, that Egypt's government and society should have centered upon a monarchic form of rule that we might call "absolute".

THE KING RULES

What better illustration could describe Egyptian government and society than a man's private farm? Here he was absolute master, and here he could produce a maximum amount of food by careful irrigation. He would brook no trespassers, and would slaughter those who threatened the operation of his estate. The king of Egypt was a god, the incarnation of the falcon Horus, descended to earth. The land of Egypt was Horus's private estate, inherited from his deceased father, Osiris, the embodiment of the fertility of the Nile. Osiris had received it as his patrimony from his father Geb, the earth; and Geb, in turn, through his father Shu, the atmosphere, from the original creator, Atum, the sun-god.

The prospective king is addressed:

Art thou Horus, the son of Osiris? Art thou the eldest god, the son of Hathor? Art thou the seed of Geb?

The king replies:

Osiris has commanded that I should appear as Horus's double. Those four spirits who are in Heliopolis have written it in the log of the two great gods in the firmament! [1] (1)

To prevent any disjunctive period of strife, the passage of power at the death of one king and the accession of his successor had to be peaceful and immediate: the king is dead, long live the king!

1. Numbers in parentheses refer to the Bibliography of texts translated, which can be found at the back of the volume.

Regnal year 6, first month of winter, day 10: the day on which the chief of police Nakht-Min came with the news 'the Hawk has flown to heaven, namely (king) Sety (II), and another now stands in his place.' (2)

Biography of Amenemheb

Now when the king had completed his life of many good years in valour, in might, and in justification, beginning with year 1 down to year 54, third month of winter, the last day—that is the reign of the Majesty of the king of Upper and Lower Egypt Menkheperre, deceased—he flew to heaven uniting with the sun-disc, the divine limbs coalescing with him who made him. And when day dawned on the morrow, and the sun-disc began to shine, and heaven was bathed in light, the king of Upper and Lower Egypt 'Okheperure the Son of the Sun, Amenhotpe (II) the god ruler of Thebes, given life! was ensconced upon the throne of his father. He lighted upon his *serekh*, seized fast the white crown, and when he had come to grips with the foes of the red crown, he cut off the heads of their chiefs, and appeared as Horus son of Isis. (3)

Since the universe, in Egyptian thought, had issued from the creator's hands in a state which could not be improved upon, the only concept of betterment that could be entertained was one of restoration. The king could only better the lot of his people by bringing back the normative condition of *ma'at* (truth, justice, order); and this could be done only if the country had retrogressed from the pristine state of *ma'at* ordained by heaven. Even though in actual fact a king might have succeeded to the throne after a most prosperous reign by his predecessor, still the stereotype of the myth must construe his coming to power as the restoration of order after anarchy. One would be hard put to it to guess that the reign in honour of which the following lines were composed, viz. that of Merneptah (c. 1224–1214 B.C.), followed the prosperous and lengthy rule of Ramesses II!

Be at ease, the entire land, (for) good times have come! The Lord—life, prosperity, health!—has arisen over all lands, and Justice has settled in place. A king of Upper and Lower Egypt, possessed of millions of years, with a great kingship like Horus . . . one who will afflict Egypt with festivals, the Son of the Sun, abler than any king . . . . Come and see! *Ma'at* has subdued Evil, and Wrong-doing has fallen flat . . . The waters rise, they do not dwindle, and the Nile brings prosperity. Days are long, the nights have hours, and the moon rises regularly. The gods are contented and happy . . . ! (4)

THE KING APPOINTS

As all power and authority resided in the king, only he could delegate it to his officials. The latter, at least in theory, owed their appointments to the king alone; but in fact the vast number of officials in the lower echelons were probably chosen by their immediate superiors under the monarch's blanket authorization. In the text translated below, Nebamun, who was to occupy an office of medium importance in the local administration of Thebes, is promoted by the king himself through the intermediary of a royal secretary.

Biographical Text of Nebamun (c. 1405 B.C.)

Regnal year 6. The command issued by the Majesty of the Palace —life, prosperity, health!—on this day to the count and commander of ships. This command reads as follows: 'Receive a good old age in favour of the king, for carrying out the business relating to the standard-bearer Nebamun of the royal ship "Beloved-of-Amun," who has reached advanced age serving Pharaoh—life, prosperity, health! —with a true heart. He is better now than he used to be in performing what is assigned to him; and he has not informed on others, nor have I found any fault in him, though he was rigorously(?) investigated. Now My Majesty—life, prosperity, health!— has commanded to appoint(?) him chief of police on the west of the city . . . until he reach a revered state; also to exempt his chattels, his cattle, his fields, his serfs, or anything of his, whether on water or land, from interference by any king's inspector . . . [The accompanying scene shows Nebamun adoring the king who sits in a kiosk, and receiving a tall standard from an officer identified by the text "The king's scribe Yuni, repeating life, came for this purpose"]. (5)

Two strong tendencies influenced the choice of officials in ancient Egypt: the need to select the ablest and best trained man for the job, and the time-honoured custom of confirming a son in his father's office. In fact little conflict arose, perhaps because of all candidates for a post, the son of the previous incumbent, who had the opportunity to learn the job from his father, was *ipso facto* the best choice. But in important offices of state the king sometimes took steps to prevent hereditary tenure. In the text translated below Ramesses II (1290–1224 B.C.) takes the unusual step of travelling to the domicile of the prospective candidate to install him in the important post of high-priest of Amun at Thebes. The king's choice was not a member of Amun's priesthood at Thebes, the obvious place to look for a new high-priest, but a cleric from the provinces; moreover, the king avers, it was not really his choice at all, but the god's, who singled out Nebwennef's name from a list drawn up and placed before him. Despite frequent reference in later Egyptian texts to decision by recourse to an oracle, we are still largely ignorant of the mechanics whereby a cult statue made its will known!

Induction of Nebwennef

Regnal year 1, third month of Inundation, after His Majesty sailed north from the southern city (i.e. Thebes) . . . . He came thence in praise, after the reception of benedictions on behalf of the life, prosperity and health of the king of Upper and Lower Egypt, Usermare Setepenre, living forever! and landed in the Abydos nome. Then was introduced into His Majesty's presence the First Prophet of Amun, Nebwennef, now deceased, although at that time he was still only First Prophet of Anhur and of Hathor mistress of Denderah, and overseer of prophets of all the gods, southward to Hraihiamun and northward to Thinis. Then said His Majesty to him: 'You are the First Prophet of Amun. His treasury and his granaries are under your seal; you are commander of his house, and all his provisions are under your charge. The temple of Hathor mistress of Denderah is under your charge as well, just as(?) are the offices of your ancestors and the post wherein you functioned formerly. As surely as Re lives for me and loves me, and my father Amun favours me! I mentioned to him (Amun) the names of every last courtier and even the commander of infantry, and then proceeded to repeat for him the names of the prophets and princes of his house who stand in his presence; but he was not satisfied with any one of them until I pronounced your name to him. Perform well for him, as he has desired you. I know that you are competent . . . . May he establish you before his house, grant you old age within it, and effect your burial in his city . . .' Thereupon the courtiers and the Council of Thirty as one man thanked the goodness of His Majesty, and kissed the earth very many times in the presence of this Good God . . . . His Majesty gave him (i.e. Nebwennef) his (Amun's) two gold seals, and his electrum sceptre. He was promoted to the office of First Prophet of Amun, overseer of the silver and gold storehouses, overseer of granaries, and of all troops and artisans in Thebes . . . (6)

THE KING ADMONISHES

The order of the universe, to the ancient Egyptian, was the same order (and justice) which informed the state and society. The same word, *ma'at*, was used for both. In Egyptian jargon, the gods and the king "lived on" this *ma'at*, and their actions were supposed to be characterized by the fairness and justice which the term implied. From his officials the king expected a similar adherence to *ma'at*, as the following instructions to a newly-appointed vizier show.

Admonition of the Vizier

Then said His Majesty to him: 'watch over the office of vizier and be vigilant concerning everything that is done in it. Lo, it is the king-pin of the entire land. Lo, as for the vizierate, it is not at all pleasant, but bitter . . . It is the bronze in a wall of gold to the house of its master. Lo, he is one who should not show favouritism to officials or councillors, nor make chattels? of any people . . . . So you must yourself see to it that everything is done in accordance with what is in the law and that everything is done exactly so . . . . Lo, as for the official who is in the public eye, water and wind report on all that he does, and lo, what he does is not unknown. Indeed, if a wrong(?) comes about(?) which he perpetrated upon another official(?) for his (sic) wrong, that he should not induct him on the word of a functionary, it will become known at the publication(?) of his decision through his saying it in the presence of the functionary in question . . . . What he does cannot be ignored. Lo, the refuge of the official is the performance of things in accordance with instructions . . . . Now this is teaching, and may you act accordingly. Regard the man whom you know the same way as the man whom you do not know, the one who has access to you like the one who lives far from your house. Lo, as for the official who acts like this, he flourishes here in this place. Do not pass over a petitioner before you have given his plea a hearing. If there be a petitioner who petitions you, do not mete out punishment(?) simply on what he has to say; but punish him only when you have informed him about what you are punishing him for . . . . Do not get angry with a man over nothing, but get angry over the thing which should provoke anger. Display your fear-inspiring qualities and you will be feared. The real official is the official who is feared. Lo, the dignity of the official is the performance(?) of *ma'at*. Lo, even if a man displays his fear-inspiring qualities a million-fold, and there be in him an element of injustice that people know about, then they do not say of him "he is a gentleman!" . . . . Lo, may you strive to perform your office, and to perform it justly. Lo, what is wanted in the conduct of a vizier is the performance of *ma'at.*' (7)

THE KING GRANTS AN AUDIENCE

The injunction to inspire fear of oneself was followed as well by the monarch in surrounding his person with a panoply commensurate with his divine dignity. Something of the awe one might have felt in the divine and august presence of the king of Upper and Lower Egypt is conveyed by the description Sinuhe gives of his audience with Senwosret I (c. 1971–1928 B.C.). Sinuhe, in exile for many years, has just returned to Egypt, and is uncertain of the reception he will receive:

Reception of Sinuhe

When day dawned one came to summon me, while ten men were coming and ten men going, to usher me into the place. I touched my head to the ground between the sphinxes. As the royal children stood in the gate to greet me, the courtiers introduced me into the broad hall and directed me to the private apartments. I found His Majesty upon the great throne in a gateway(?) of electrum. At once I was stretched flat on my belly, I forgot myself in his presence. This god (i.e. the king) addressed me in friendly fashion, but I was like a man seized at night-time: my soul was gone, my limbs trembled, my heart it was not in my body that I should distinguish life from death. Thereupon His Majesty said to one of these courtiers: 'Pick him up! Make him speak to me.' Then said His Majesty: 'Behold, you are come, after journey in flight through foreign lands! Old age has attacked you, feebleness has caught up with you. Your body's burial is no small affair: you should not be buried by nomads, no, no indeed you shouldn't! You do not speak when your name is pronounced. Are you afraid of being punished?' I made a terrified response: 'What does my Lord say to me? If I (must) answer it, (then my answer would be): it was not my doing, but indeed it was the hand of god. In my belly is a terror like that which gave rise to the fated flight! Behold, I am before thee. Life belongs to thee. May Thy Majesty do as he wishes.' Thereupon the royal children were ushered in, and His Majesty said to the queen: 'Look, here is Sinuhe, come as an Asiatic, a creation of the nomads!' She uttered a very great cry, and all the royal children squealed together. They said to His Majesty: 'It is not really he, O Sovereign, my Lord!' Said His Majesty: 'It is really he!' (8)

> The following text describes the reception of booty from a foreign campaign during the reign of Amenhotpe II (1438–1412 B.C.). The emphatic denial—that such a thing has not been seen since remote antiquity ("since the ancestors who existed formerly")—is typical of Egyptian hyperbole.

Review of Tribute

His Majesty appeared in the midst of Thebes upon the great dais to view(?) the marvels of this army, the captured booty of the first(?) victorious campaign of the Lord of the Two Lands. Then this army brought in the tribute of the southern countries, into the presence of this Good God, while the court gave praise, and this army thanked His Majesty, saying: 'Great is thy power, O thou Good God . . . Greater is this tribute than that of any other foreign lands, it has not been witnessed since the ancestors who existed formerly; but it has happened to thee, O our Lord!' Tally of those who bear this tribute:

Those laden with . . . ,	200 men;
those laden with gold,	150 men;
those laden with carnelian,	200 men;
those laden with ivory,	340 men;
those laden with ebony,	1,000 men;
those laden with various fine aromatics of the southern countries,	200 men;
those laden with . . . wood,	34 men;
those with live panthers,	10 men;

those with hounds,	20 men;
those with long- and short-horned cattle,	400 men;
Total of those with this tribute,	2,657 men. (9)

THE KING COMMANDS

The tradition of Pharaonic kingship and all that it implied was unwritten. There was no "constitution," nor, as far as we know, was there any law code. But very often unwritten custom is far stronger and more binding on those who practise it than codified law, for any law reduced to writing has *ipso facto* sacrificed a good deal of its spirit to the letter of the word and simply invites circumvention by devious "legalities." What we might call civil law, in Egyptian "the laws of the country," was largely based on a vast store of precedent which belonged to the realm of oral tradition. In contrast, the "king's laws" were formally written out on papyrus, sealed in the king's presence, and later published in stone for all to see. These are the royal edicts ("king's-commands") which deal *ad hoc* with problems of the day, and constitute injunctions, directives, prohibitions, and the setting of penalties and exemptions. In the following example from the long reign of Pepy II (c. 2286–2190 B.C.) the king exempts the entire staff of a temple estate at Koptos (modern Qift, c. 300 miles south of Cairo) from recruitment on royal labour projects.

Horus Netjery-kha'u. The year after the 11th occurrence of the Numbering, 2nd month of *shomu*, day 26.

Royal decree to the superintendent of the Pyramid City, chancellor, the honorable vizier and superintendent of the royal secretariat, Dja'u; to the count and governor of Upper Egypt, Khuy; to the bishop; to the supervisors(?) of priests; to the chief officers of the Double-Falcon township.

With respect to the god Min of Koptos in the Double-Falcon township, and the bishop, supervisor(?) of priests, all the chattels of the property of the house of Min, the acolytes who serve Min, the day-staff(?) of the work house, and the builders of this temple, who are therein: My Majesty does not permit their being put to work in the royal herds, in the cattle-pastures, in the ass- or goat-pastures . . . in any service or any tasks which are assigned from the King's-house, throughout all eternity. They are exempted for Min of Koptos, valid from to-day(?), by explicit command of the king of Upper and Lower Egypt Neferkare, living forever and ever.

As for any governor of Upper Egypt who may effect their recruitment, or any chief officer . . . who may actively recruit and take them, for the Department of king's recruits, or the Department of agriculture, or the archives, or the office of sealed documents, or may put them to any work of the King's-house, he is one who has committed a crime of treason.

As for any local recruitment-order which is brought before the governor of Upper Egypt to be put into effect, after it has been brought before the magistrates, My Majesty commands that he (the governor) should expunge the name of the priest or acolyte in question (i.e the one who issued the order) of this temple . . . .

The King of Upper and Lower Egypt Neferkare, living for ever and ever, has commanded publication(?) should be made of this decree, by putting it on a stone stela set at the gate of Min of Koptos in the Double-Falcon township for the acolytes of this township to see, that they may never recruit these priests for any work of the King's-house in the course of eternity for ever and ever . . . . Sealed in the presence of the king himself. (10)

The precise penalty to be meted out to the luckless official who inscribed the name of some priest of Min on a labour roll, either by design or inadvertently, is not here prescribed. Nor is it certain whether, as was the king's wish, the edict was honoured for all time. The probability, however, is that with the passing of the monarch whose seal rendered a particular decree binding, the rulings set forth in the document would fall into desuetude, (as in fact would the king's other memorials, his monuments, buildings and even his tomb).

THE KING CONFIDES

By far the majority of texts from Ancient Egypt speak of the king as the god on earth, and clothe him in the mythological symbols discussed above. Only rarely can we get behind the stereotyped façade and come into contact with the personality of the "Horus-king." One document which helps us in this regard is the so-called "Instruction for Merikare," which purports to be the advice given by an aged king at the end of his life to his son and heir apparent, one Merikare (c. 2080 B.C.), on how to govern. Such "instructions" are fairly common in Egyptian literature, and in keeping with the practice in other fields of Near Eastern research, are usually classed under the general heading of "Wisdom texts." But it is not "wisdom" in our sense of the word, but rather "lifemanship" expounded in the same vein as the Biblical Book of Proverbs. An old man, on the point of departing this life, takes his son aside and gives him some good, practical advice on how to get ahead in the world. If he had lived in more modern times, the writer of an ancient "Wisdom" work might have entitled his product "How to Win Friends and Influence People," for this is precisely the burden of such "Teachings."

"The Instruction for Merikare," in contrast to most Wisdom texts, is designed for a limited audience. Since it is a dissertation on statecraft, it is directed towards only those who will one day become king. There is no more revealing text with regard to what sort of man the Egyptians thought their king should be, and by what sort of conduct he should run the country.

. . . If you encounter a townsman whose deed is a transgression against you, lay a suit against him before the court; crush him, for he is an enemy. An orator is the scum of the city. Curb the rabble and force the heat out of them without getting unduly angry with them. As for the enemy who is poor, he spreads hostility, the pauper it is that causes trouble. The army which proves unruly(?) let them end up eating(?) . . . when the rabble grows angry, let them into the storehouse. . . . Be just in the sight of god . . .

Get skill in words so that you may be strong . . . words are stouter than any weapon, and the trained mind cannot be taken advantage of . . .

Emulate your fathers, your ancestors . . . behold, their words abide in writing; open and read that you may attain to knowledge. The skilled man develops only through having been taught. Do not be evil, kindness is best; make your monuments endure through love of you . . . thanks is given for rewards, and they will pray for your health first and foremost.

Respect your officers, prosper your people; make fast your frontiers and boundaries, for it is a good thing to act for the future. Respect the lively, alert person, but the dull-witted is a miserable fellow . . .

Exalt your officers that they may perform your laws. One who is rich in his own house does not show partiality, an owner of property is one who lacks not. But the pauper does not speak what he knows is true, and he who says 'Oh that I had . . . !' is not straightforward. He shows partiality to him whom he loves, and leans towards him who has bribes. Great is a great man whose great ones are great, and strong the king who has courtiers, and wealthy the man rich in great men. You should speak the truth in your house, that the great men who are in the land may fear you. Things go normally for the straight-forward lord; it is the front of the house (i.e. the master's quarters) that instills fear in the back (i.e. the servants' quarters).

Act justly that you may endure on earth. Quiet the weeper, oppress not the widow, do not deprive a man of his paternal property, do no harm to officials on their own land. Beware of punishing wrongfully, do not kill—it is of no advantage to you. Punish rather with flogging and imprisonment, and thus will the land be stabilized. Judge the enemy whose plottings have been found out; God knows the refractory and God condemns him to a bloody end(?) . . . Do not kill a man whose ability you know, one with whom long ago you recited the writings (i.e. a schoolmate) . . .

Levy your draftees that the Residence may love you, increase your adherents from the present generation. See! Your cities are filled with new recruits. Twenty years it is that the youth are at ease in pursuit of their desire; then a new generation comes forth on the heels of its predecessor(?) . . . . Enrich your officials, promote your fighting men, increase the numbers of the levies of your retainers; let them be provided with various things, endowed with fields and presented with cattle.

Do not distinguish between a gentleman's son and a commoner; take a man unto yourself because of his ability, that all tasks of skill may be performed . . . Protect your frontier, raise up your monuments: a work-gang is useful to him who possesses it. Make monuments for God: the result is to perpetuate the name of him who does it. A man ought to do what is beneficial to his *bai:* monthly service as a priest, wearing white sandals, going to the temple, discretion(?) regarding the mysteries, entering the shrine, eating bread in the temple.

. . . He-of-the-Two-Banks (the king) is a wise man, the king who possesses courtiers cannot be foolish. He was intelligent (even) when he emerged from the womb, and God has elevated him over millions of men.

Kingship is a fine office. It has no son or brother to be perpetuated upon its monuments, but one carries on from another; a man acts on his predecessor's behalf, in order that what he has done may be carried on by another who comes after him . . . (11)

Underlying the discourse of this Egyptian Machiavelli is the sober realisation that the King of Upper and Lower Egypt, divine and omnipotent as he may be, can yet be the centre of factional strife. He, as well as the administration of which he was the cornerstone, constituted for Egyptian society the only barrier between order and chaos.

2

"Extending the Boundaries"

Egyptian Imperialism

Lo, the miserable Asiatic! It's a difficult life in the place where he is, suffering from lack of water, hidden by many trees, the paths thereof difficult because of mountains. He does not reside in one place, but the tracks of his feet wander around. He has been fighting since the time of Horus, without conquering nor yet being conquered. He does not announce a day for fighting, like an outlawed thief of a gang (of thieves?). (1)

. . . I am a king who speaks and acts; what my heart decides, that is what comes to pass through my own agency; I am aggressive to conquer, a lucky dare-devil, who does not allow a matter to rest in his heart (i.e. is not indecisive); who thinks for his dependents and is usually lenient, but who is not lenient toward the enemy who has attacked him; attacking when he is attacked, desisting when they desist, retaliating in accordance to the proportion of the matter. Because, as for him who holds back after being attacked,

15

he is one that strengthens the heart of the enemy. Aggressiveness is victory, retreat is defeat; the true coward is he who is pushed back from his own frontier. For the Nubian has but to hear (i.e., a sound) in order to fall at a word! It is merely answering him that causes him to retreat, being aggressive towards him causes him to turn tail. When one retreats, he again shows aggressiveness. They are not people to be respected, they are craven-hearted wretches. My Majesty has seen them: it is no lie! (2)

The king is destroyer(?) of Naharin, who sealed the fate of Pakhaty, the one who . . . the mistress(?) in Sangar, the maidservant in Byblos, the little girl of Alalakh and the old woman of Arapkha. And as for the people of Takhsi, they're all useless; really, what are they good for? Another message for the viceroy: don't be easy with the Nubians at all. Beware of their people and their magicians. See to the labour of the freeholders, which you shall bring to deliver to the official. . . . Don't listen to their words, and don't meddle in their affairs! (3)

The feeling of disgust with foreign ways and self-conscious apprehension is very marked in these texts emanating for the circle of the king. For the Egyptian ruler the Asiatic and the Nubian were troublesome groups, just beyond the range of effectual control. He had set up a tightly-organized and (usually) efficient administration which depended largely on the complete subservience of the inhabitants of the land to a central authority. Sedentary occupation and control through resident agents were prerequisites of such a system; but the nomad cherished freedom of movement and immunity to controls. And in the texts translated above it is these characteristics which rankle the most.

If the Asiatic and the Nubian on the one hand and the Egyptian on the other could have lived their lives without impinging on the other's territorial sphere, all would have been well. But the "modern" sophisticated nation-state depended heavily on access to mines, quarries, and trading centres which lay in the territory of the nomad; and the latter for his part was irresistibly drawn toward the Nile Valley to tap the resources in land, food, and goods which the nation-state had produced. Small wonder that the confrontation in the graphic and literary tradition of the Egyptians (the only side capable ideologically and culturally of conceiving and recording universals) should have conformed itself to the motif of the world-ruler trying to impose law and order on a lesser, congenitally immoral, breed of barbarians.

Consequently we encounter, as early as the First Dynasty, and especially on rock surfaces close to the Sinai mines, the oft-repeated motif of the king smiting a falling Bedouin. The accompanying text will record some such act as "Horus smites the foreign lands," the whole presentation being partly record, partly apotropaic gesture. As a projection of the royal obligation epithets are often appended to divine names signifying the same punitive activity towards the wretched aliens: "Sopdu who smites the Mentiu," "Horus lord of foreign lands," "Horus who is over foreign lands," "Thoth lord of the (foreign) bowmen."

Entry into Egypt was at most periods closely watched, and frontier guards were obliged to keep records of arrivals and departures.

The scribe Anen writes to his lord the scribe of the treasury Kageb . . . . We have completed the admittance of the tribes of the bedu of Edom through the keep of Merneptah-satisfied-with-ma'at, which is in Succoth, destined for the wells of the House of Atum of Merneptah-satisfied-with-ma'at, which is in Succoth, to sustain their herds, through the mighty *ku* of Pharaoh, l.p.h., the good sun of every land; in the year 8, epagomenal day 5, viz. the Birth of Seth. I sent a copy (of their names) to the place where my lord is, together with other specific days on which admittance may be had through the keep of Merneptah-satisfied-with-ma'at, which is in Succoth . . . (4)

By a process of externalizing the problem in a manner which seems rather modern, the Egyptians were wont to ascribe the

troubles of those periods of their history characterized by political and economic weakness to the incursions of foreign
elements. Thus what was really a result, or at worst a con-
comitant—when the government is weak the frontier is apt
to be left undefended—comes close to being elevated to the
status of a major factor. The distress of the First Intermediate
Period is thus described by an early Middle Kingdom document:

The Prophecy of Neferty

The lector priest Neferty . . . pondered what had happened in
the land, and recalled the state(?) of the East. For Asiatics were on
the move in their strength and were setting terror in the hearts of
those who were harvesting and seizing the teams which were plow-
ing. He said, 'Up my heart! and beweep this land wherein you began.
To be silent is to cover up(?), because what is said about it is something to be taken seriously, and because now the official is one
denigrated in the land wherein you began. Do not be listless! See,
it is before your eyes! Face up to what is in front of you! See now,
there are no more officials in the present state of the land. What
was accomplished is as that which was never accomplished, as it
were at the outset of Re's creation. The land has completely gone
to ruin without exception . . . This land is destroyed, and nobody
thinks of it, nobody speaks of it, nobody weeps for it. What is the
land like? The sun-disc is clouded over and does not shine that
mankind may see. People cannot live if the storm clouds come over
. . . . The river of Egypt is empty, and the water is crossed on foot.
Water will have to be looked for for the ships to sail on, for its normal course has become a sand-bank, while the normal sand-banks
have become water: the fluid turns into the solid. The southwind
shall oppose the northwind, and heaven has no single breeze. A foreign bird shall lay in the marshes of the Delta, having built its nest
beside the inhabitants: it brings people closer to want. Destroyed indeed is that beneficence of the fish-pools, and those who bore the
fish knives, laden down with fish and fowl. All good things are
gone, and the land cast down in distress because of those food

needs of the barbarians who are everywhere in the land. Enemies appear on the east, the Asiatics will descend into Egypt. A fort will be breached even though another is nearby, for its garrison will not listen. The seige ladder will be run up(?) in the night, the fort will be entered, the ramparts scaled(?), while everyone sleeps and he who reclines says 'I am on watch!' Wild game will drink at the rivers of Egypt, they will refresh themselves upon their banks through lack of anyone to drive them away!' (5)

No matter whether the speaker credits the Asiatics with siege techniques which we might doubt they actually knew of and could use, the Egyptian fear is nonetheless a real one. Concern over such a lawless and potentially destructive element led Egyptian kings of all periods not only to fortify their frontiers, but also to engage in what we today would call pre-emptive strikes. In the Old Kingdom and First Intermediate Period the catchwords were "pacification" and "placing the fear of Horus in the foreign lands."
Biography of Pepy-nakht, governor of Elephantine, under Pepy II, 23rd cent. B.C.:

Overseer of the pyramid city Pepy-men-nofer, unique friend, lector priest, commander of aliens, who brings the products of foreign lands to his lord . . . who places the fear of Horus in the foreign lands . . . revered before the great god, Pepy-nakht . . . . Now the Majesty of my lord sent me to pacify these foreign lands (certain districts in Nubia are meant), and I did so more efficiently than anything, to the praise of my lord. I brought two chiefs of these foreign lands to the royal residence with peace offerings of long horns, short horns, and goats . . . And the Majesty of my lord sent me to the land of the Asiatic to fetch him (the corpse of) the unique friend, skipper and commander of aliens . . . who had been building a 'Byblos'-boat there to go to Pwenet; for the Asiatics who are over the sand had slain him together with the army corps that was with him. (6)

Akhtoy, in instructing his son Merikare, describes how he restored the Delta to his kingdom:

Then I came to the throne as a lord in the city whose heart was distraught over the Delta . . . I pacified the entire West as far as the seacoast; now it works for us(?) and produces *mrw*-wood, and when *w'n*-wood is available they give it to us. The East is rich in barbarians, but they work on . . . ; the islands in the middle have come back and every man within them . . . now the barbarians are confined by sealed fortifications, for I made the Delta smite them, and I plundered their chattels, and seized their cattle, for the Asiatics' abominable acts against Egypt. Do not be concerned about it. The Asiatic is a crocodile on his river-bank: he snaps at the single wayfarer, but does not attempt the district of the populous city. (7)

The basic commercial interest in the products of foreign countries is strongly marked in many texts. Freedom of access to raw materials, the diligence of the king's agent in seeking them out, "showing the flag" in foreign climes, punitive treatment of native opposition, even the organization of a foreign labour force—these are the themes which the Egyptian official charged with enterprise abroad dwells upon in his biographical inscriptions.

Yebya' (18th cent. B.C.): The hereditary prince and count, the deputy overseer of the treasury, Yebya' . . . one whom the king sent to open up Kush, so efficient was he in the king's opinion; who sets the awe of the Lord of the Two Lands in the midst of rebellious foreign countries, accompanying the Sovereign's monuments to far-off foreign lands. (8)

The treasurer Sobekhotpe (Amenemhet III, late 19th cent. B.C.): one trusted by the king in missions to foreign lands to bring precious stones to His Majesty. (9)

Amenemhet (same reign): the commander of infantry, Amenemhet . . . who smote the Nubian, and opened the door of the land of the Asiatic, who penetrated every foreign land. (10)

Hetepy (same reign): one who opened the doors of foreign lands at the instigation of his lord, in accordance with the counsel given him. (11)

Ptah-wer (same reign): the treasurer, who directs multitudes in an alien land . . . who binds(?) Asia for him who is in the palace, who reaches the limits of foreign lands on foot, penetrating difficult valleys . . . (12)

The intestine strife of the First Intermediate Period had made Egyptians sensitive to the potential fluidity of territorial boundaries. Side by side with the older concept of restoring peace as a re-union of two entities, we encounter restoration under the guise of pushing back the frontiers of a centrally-located principality. Building frontier forts was an essentially static and defensive exercise: extending the frontier removed the potential trouble spot far from the home counties. Of Senwosret I the exile Sinuhe sings to an Asiatic chief:

Sinuhe, B70ff: how joyful is this land now that he has assumed the rule! He is one who extends the boundaries, he will seize the southern lands, he will not trifle with the northern countries; he was made to smite the savages and to trample upon the desert nomads. Go to him, let him know your name! Don't curse His Majesty from afar. He will not fail to do good to the foreign land which shall be loyal to him. (13)

The Hyksos invasion (c. 1665 B.C.) was, for Egypt, a realization of the worst fears which had motivated her previous posture towards foreigners. Moreover, the incursion was not a desultory wandering of a handful of dirty nomads, but a take-over of part of the country by a people as sophisticated and highly organized as the Egyptians themselves. The following record (originally on two stelae set up in the temple of Amun at Thebes) was inscribed at the behest of king Kamose (died c. 1558 B.C.) who was instrumental in prosecuting the war of liberation against the Hyksos. The feeling of humiliation and outrage at seeing part of his land in enemy hands is strongly marked in the text.

First Kamose Stela:
. . . His Majesty debated in his palace with his council of officials which was in his train: 'In what way can he be aware of my strength, viz. the prince who is in Avaris, or the other who is in Kush? I sit here associated with an Asiatic and a Nubian, each one having his slice of Egypt . . . a man cannot dwell properly when despoiled by the taxes of the savages! I am going to come to grips with him, and break his body; my desire is to save Egypt which the Asiatics have smitten!' The officials of his council said: 'Look, they are loyal to the Asiatics as far as Kusae, and they have pulled out their tongues altogether. We are at ease in possession of our part of Egypt, Elephantine is strong, and the central region is with us as far as Kusae. Their fallow(?) fields are plowed for us, our cattle are in the Delta marshes, and barley is sent for our swine. Our cattle have not been seized. . . . He has the land of the Asiatic, we have Egypt. When there is some move against us, only then should we act against him.' But they offended His Majesty . . .

Kamose disregards his council's advice, and leads his army against the Hyksos. Crossing the border at Kusae, he attacks an Egyptian vassal of the Hyksos in Middle Egypt:

As for Tety the son of Pepy, who was in Nefrusy, I did not let him escape. . . . I spent the night in my ship, my heart happy; at dawn I was upon him like a hawk. It happened about breakfast time . . . I hacked down his wall, I slaughtered his people, I caused his wife to descend to the river bank. My army were like lions with the spoil: slaves, cattle, milk, fat, honey, dividing their possessions, their hearts happy. (14)
Second Kamose Stela:
(Kamose has laid seige to Avaris, the Hyksos capital in the north-

eastern Delta, and is addressing the Hyksos king Apophis) 'An evil report is in the midst of your town, that you have been thrown back to the side of your army! Your authority is restricted, now that you have made me a prince, while you are a ruler who is asking for the block of execution on which you will fall! Look behind you! My army has your rear in difficulties. The ladies of Avaris will not conceive, their hearts will not stir in their bellies when they hear the war-hoop of my troops!' I was moored at Per-Djedken, my heart happy, for I had given Apophis a bad time, that weak-armed prince of Syria who thinks big things in his heart which never come to pass for him! . . . I spied his wives upon his roof, peering out of his windows . . . they did not stir at all(?) when they saw me; they peered out of their harim on their walls, like fledgling chicks in their holes, and said 'He's a fast one!' Behold, I am come, and the time is right for me, my time is opportune. As the mighty Amun endures! I shall not leave you, I shall not let you walk the fields, even when I am not here with you! Does your heart fail, O miserable Asiatic? I am drinking of the wine of your vineyards, which the Asiatics whom I captured trod out for me . . . All the good products of Syria, I seized them all. I left nothing belonging to Avaris, so that(?) she is empty, and the Asiatic perished. Does your heart fail, O miserable Asiatic, you who used to say 'I am lord without rival from Hermopolis as far as Pi Hathor on the banks of Avaris, in the two rivers'? I left it devastated, without people therein, hacking up their cities, demolishing their cult-places, turning them into charred ruins for ever, on account of the destruction they had wrought in the midst of Egypt. For they had allowed themselves to hear the call of the Asiatics, and had forsaken Egypt, their mistress . . . (15)

In the wake of the expulsion of the Hyksos the Egyptian armies pursued the initiative and within a century had secured a territory which (according to the Egyptians themselves) extended from Karoy in the Sudan to the Euphrates. In rationalizing this new phenomenon of empire, the texts speak as of old of "extending the frontiers," the implication being that the land taken was not considered as conquered units, but territory absorbed into an expanding homeland. Justification for conquest was found in various casuistries: sometimes the texts aver, as they had in the earlier periods, that it was Pharaoh's obligation to quell disturbances perpetrated by the barbarians on the border; much more frequently, however, the imperialist campaigns are passed off as retaliation against barbarians who had attacked Egypt. Occasionally the inscriptions employ the romantic image (at home in an heroic age, which is for the most part alien to Egypt) of the warlike hero who loves a good fight; less often do they insist on the nationalistic urge to make Egypt "top dog." Finally, there is the strong tendency to translate the reason for the wars into the realm of the gods: Amun or the Sun-god had directed the king to go and conquer his neighbours, and had given him title to all the foreign countries.

Tombos Stela of Thutmose I, c. 1511 B.C.:

Regnal year 2, 2nd month of Inundation, day 15, under the Majesty of . . . the king of Upper and Lower Egypt 'Okheperkare, given life, the son of Re, Thutmose . . . , being the second year after he was inducted and rose to power as overlord of the Two Lands, to rule what the sun-disc encircles, viz. the Southland and the Northland, from the limits of the 'Portions' of the Two Lands; when, at the Union of the Two Lands, he sat upon the throne of Geb, and the crowns and the mighty double diadem were elevated.

Now His Majesty had taken his inheritance and had seated himself upon the dais of Horus in order to extend the frontiers of Thebes, the property of She-who-Faces-Her-Lord, to enslave the dirty ones, the foreigners, and those whom the god detests, the Hau-nebu . . . . The southerners come north and the northerners come south, and all lands together bear their tribute to the Good God, the primordial king, 'Okheperkare, may he live eternally.

Victorious is Horus, Lord of the Two Lands! He has tied up the . . . (?), their towns are his in utter subservience; the skin-clad(?) people tramp on foot to His Majesty and bow low to Her-that-is-in-his-forehead. He has felled the chief of the Nubians, and the negro withers and chokes in his grasp, for he has taken over the boundaries of his two sides. There was no escape for the recalcitrant ones who had contravened his protection, not one of them was spared; the Nubian bowmen fell to his slaughter and were laid prostrate throughout their lands; their gore inundated their valleys, the mouths of which were worn smooth(?) as with a cloudburst of driving rain. The carrions were overhead, a host of birds, picking and carrying away, and the crocodile fastened himself to the fugitive who had hidden himself from the stout-armed Horus . . . fortress of his entire army, who turns facing the Nine Bows together, like a young panther in a herd at rest.

The power of His Majesty blinded them, he who had attained the limits of the earth in its breadth, who had trod its extremities in his victorious might seeking battle, but finding no-one who would face him; he who had broken into valleys which the ancestors had not known, and the former wearers of the 'Two Ladies' had not seen. His southern boundary is at the forefront of this land (i.e. Nubia), his northern at that encircling stream in which the current flows southward (i.e. the Euphrates). Nothing like this happened to former kings! His name has reached the circumference of the sky . . . the oath is taken in his name in all lands, so great is his power! It has not been seen in the annals of past kings since the Followers of Horus.

Breath is granted by him to the one who follows him, his largess goes to him that adheres to his path. Lo, His Majesty is Horus who has seized upon his kingship of millions of years, the islands of the Ocean are subservient to him, and the entire earth is under his feet . . . ! (16)

The following text is the record of a speech by Thutmose III to his court, in which he recounts (not in chronological order) some incidents from his campaigns in Palestine and Syria, along with ruminations on himself, Egypt's status, and god's role. Occasionally the scribe who wrote it up breaks in with a eulogizing aside.

Gebel Barkal stela, 47th year of Thutmose III (c. 1443 B.C.):

. . . the Good God who seizes with his arm, who smites the southerners and decapitates the northerners, who lops off the heads of the bad scruffies, and makes slaughter of the Montiu of Asia, who overthrows those of the dirty ones who rebel, and ties up the lands of the ends of the world, who smites the bowmen of Nubia and reaches the limits of those foreign lands which had attacked him. He is one who faces the fray, raging . . . . He is a king who fights by himself, to whom a multitude is of no concern; for he is abler than a million men in a vast army. No equal to him has been found, a fighter aggressive on the battlefield, within whose scope no one stands; one who overpowers every foreign land in short order at the head of his army. He flashes across the two arcs of heaven like a star crossing the sky, plunging into the thick ranks; whose breath lashes out at them as a fire, turning them into something that had never existed, wallowing in their blood.

THE KING NOW REMINISCES ABOUT HIS EIGHTH CAMPAIGN

They had no champion in that land of Naharin, whose lord had abandoned it through fear. I destroyed his cities and his towns, and set them on fire; My Majesty made them into ruins which shall never be founded again. I plundered all their inhabitants who were taken away as prisoners of war, their numberless cattle and their goods likewise. I took away the provisions from them, and pulled up their corn; I cut down all their trees, even all their fruit trees, and their districts are now wind-blown(?). My Majesty destroyed it, and it is now become burnt dust on which foliage will never grow again.

Now when My Majesty crossed over to the marshes of Asia, I had many ships constructed of cedar upon the mountains of God's-land, in the vicinity of the Lady of Byblos, and placed upon carts with oxen drawing them. They travelled in the van of My Majesty to ferry my army across that great river which flows between this country and Naharin.

THE SCRIBE'S COMMENT

A king indeed to be boasted of, for the prowess of his arms in battle! One who crosses the Great Bender in pursuit of him who attacked him at the head of his army, seeking that vile doomed one throughout the lands of Mitanni. But he had fled before His Majesty to another land, a distant place, through fear.

THE KING REMINISCES ABOUT HIS
ELEPHANT HUNT

Another victorious accomplishment which Re ordained for me, when he granted me another great triumph at the swamp(?) of Niya: he allowed me to bag several lots of elephants. My Majesty fought them in herds of 120. Never had the like been done by any king since the time of the god, even by those who of old had received the white crown. I say this without boasting or exaggeration in any of it; for I did it in accordance with what Amun-re who directs My Majesty on the right road by his good counsels, ordained for me . . .

THE KING REMINISCES ABOUT HIS
FIRST CAMPAIGN

I will tell you something else: listen, O people! On my first campaign he commended to me the lands of Syria which had come to grapple with My Majesty by the hundreds of thousands and by the millions, the very best of every foreign country. Mounted on their chariots were 330 chiefs, each with his own army: lo, they were in the Kina Valley, ready at the narrow pass. But good fortune was with me where they were concerned; for when My Majesty charged them, they fled at once, falling over one another in their haste to enter Megiddo. My Majesty beseiged them for a period of seven months, before they came out . . . . Then that doomed one (i.e. the king of Kadesh, ringleader of the enemy) together with the chiefs that were with him made all their children come forth to My Majesty, bearing much tribute of gold, silver, all their horses that they had, their chariots, chariots of gold, silver, and those which were only painted, all their coats of mail, their bows, their arrows and all their weapons of war with which they had come from afar to fight against My Majesty. Now they were bringing them as tribute to My Majesty, while they stood upon their walls, hailing My Majesty, and asking that the breath of life be given them. So My Majesty had them take the oath as follows: 'We will not again act evilly against Menkheperre, given life, our lord, in our lifetime . . .' It was my father Amun that did it; it was not the hand of man! Then My Majesty let them go back to their cities, and all of them rode off on donkeys, for I had taken their horses. I took their townsmen as plunder to Egypt, and their goods likewise . . . (17)

Like Egypt proper, the new principalities engulfed by the extension of the frontiers were burdened with a tax quota, which the Egyptians pompously call tribute. Minmose, an official of Thutmose III, describes how he assessed the annual levy:

I trod Upper Syria in the following of my lord, and I assessed the levy of Upper Syria in silver, gold, lapis, various costly stones, chariots and horses without number, and herds and flocks in their multitudes. I acquainted the chiefs of Syria with their compulsory yearly labour. I assessed the levy of the chiefs of the land of Nubia in electrum . . . in gold, ivory, ebony and numerous ships of *dom*-wood: this is the levy of each year, like that of the dependents of his palace . . . (18)

Asiatics brought as captives from military campaigns were assigned in large numbers to be cultivators on temple estates.

The following text describes the Asiatics attached to Amen-hotpe III's mortuary temple at Thebes (c. 1375 B.C.):

Its (the temple's) work-house is filled with male and female slaves, consisting of the children of the chiefs of every foreign land which His Majesty took as plunder; its store-houses are stocked with every good thing the number of which is unknown, the temple itself being surrounded by the towns of Palestine, settled by the chiefs' children . . . (19)

Once in Egypt, the foreign captive was enrolled by an agency set up to record and control his whereabouts, and placed under the supervision of a priest or official. The following private letter describes the difficulty one scribe encountered in trying to track down a Syrian cultivator who had somehow gone astray:

The scribe of libations Bakenamun to the prophet Ramose of the House of Thoth . . . 'I have read the greetings you sent me; it is Re and Ptah who greet you. But I do not know whether my boy reached you. To Sekhem-pehty I sent him, and with him I despatched to you a letter. So do not hesitate in writing me at once, that I may hear how you are.

I have made enquiry about the Syrian of the House of Thoth concerning whom you wrote me. It found that, as one of the slaves of the shipment brought by the fortress commander, he was assigned to be a cultivator of the House of Thoth under your charge, in regnal year 3, 2nd. month of Harvest, day 10. For your information, his name is the Syrian Naqedy, son of Salulat, his mother being Qedy of the land of Arvad, a slave of the shipment to this house in the ship of captain Kul. His keeper said "it was the chief herald of the army, Kha-em-ope of pharaoh's garrison that received him in order to make his assignment(?)." I then went to the chief herald of the army, Kha-em-ope, of pharaoh's garrison, and he denied it, saying to me expressly(?) "it was the vizier, Meryseklimet, that received him, in order to make his assignment(?)." So I went to the vizier Merysekhmet, and he and his scribes denied it, saying "we have not seen him!" Today I have sought out the chief of the *s³kt,* saying "hand over the Syrian cultivator of the House of Thoth whom you received, in order to return him to his priest"; and I am contending at law with him, before the great court . . .' (20)

Warriors who had distinguished themselves on the battlefield, especially at the outset of the New Kingdom, were allowed to keep the enemy soldiers they had captured. The following document shows that, at least in some quarters, intermarriage was not frowned upon:

Regnal year 27 (c. 1464 B.C.) under the Majesty of the king of Upper and Lower Egypt, Menkheperre, given life and stability like Re, Thutmose-ruler-of-truth, like Re forever. Petition made by the king's barber Si-Bast, before the 'Children of the Royal Harim' as follows: 'the servant reckoned as my property whose name is Iwy-Amun, I captured him by myself, while I was following the Ruler (i.e. on military service, probably in Asia). . . . He shall not be beaten, he shall not be turned away from any royal portal. I have given him my sister Nebto's daughter whose name is Takmenet to wife. A division (i.e. of the inheritance) shall be made for her along with my wife and sister, both the same. He shall go out, but not empty. If he . . . , or if he makes a . . . against my sister, no one shall be entitled to interfere with him forever.' This writing was done . . . in the presence of . . . (there follows a list of five witnesses). (21)

3

"The Land Spins Round"

Egyptian Revolution

What happens when a tightly-organized and regimented state such as Pharaonic Egypt suffers a removal of all controls? What happens when the authority of the state can neither impose nor create the climate of acceptance for sanctions? What happens when a people who have always had good reason to expect the wisest and most effective leadership suddenly find themselves in a literal state of anarchy?

In fact, on several occasions in their long history, the Egyptians woke up to discover that this predicament had come upon them. At the close of the Old Kingdom, for reasons that are obscure, Egypt experienced a spectacular economic collapse which affected both body politic and body social. The lamentable condition of the land is described in a fragmentary text called "the Admonitions of Ipuwer," an otherwise unknown worthy who is here represented as speaking to the "Eternal Lord," an epithet usually applied to the sun-god. The description is organized into sections, usually a single stich in length, each beginning with the same deictic expression. Section is related to adjacent section in a loose way, either by similarity of content, or by punning on homonyms.

Ipuwer's lament has a curiously modern ring. The vignettes he sketches can be epitomized by formulae familiar to us all: class struggle, revolt of the workers, bankruptcy of the well-to-do, seizure of the wealth of the upper class by the masses, declining birth-rate, prevalence of suicide, falling off of revenue from foreign trade, unrestricted immigration, absence of law and order, reliance on vigilante groups, inter-county strife, refusal to pay taxes, moral bankruptcy on the part of the chief of state.

. . . the doormen say 'Let us go and plunder!' The confectioners say '. . . .', the washerman does not intend(?) to carry his load . . . ., the bird-catchers have mustered battalions . . . ., the marshes are under arms, the brewers . . . . greed(?), a man looks on his own son as his enemy; uproar is everywhere(?), and one says to another 'Come with (your) weapon!' . . . . A man goes to plough with his shield . . .

Really, the Inundation floods, but no one cultivates for it; all men say 'We do not know what may happen throughout the land.'

Really, women are sterile, they do not conceive: Khnum cannot create because of the condition of the land.

Really, the poor have become the owners of luxuries: he who never made sandals for himself is now the possessor of riches.

Really, their slaves' hearts are greedy; officials do not fraternize with their people in jocular fashion(?).

Really, the heart is aggressive, plague is throughout the land, blood is everywhere, death gives no offence. . . .

Really, many dead are buried in the river, the stream is a tomb, indeed the embalming-place has become the stream.

Really, the rich are in mourning, while the poor rejoice; every city says 'Let us drive out the influential from among us!'

Really, men are like ibises, dirt is throughout the land; there is really no one with clean clothes nowadays.

Really, the land spins round as does a potter's wheel: the robber is a possessor of riches, the upright(?) is become a thief.

. . . . Really, the river is blood: when it is drunk it repels men, and they thirst for water.

Really, gates, pillars and walls are consumed by fire, while the enclosure of the king's house, L.P.H., remains firm and enduring.

Really, the ship of the southerners is off course, towns are hacked up, Upper Egypt is become a waste land.

Really, crocodiles are surrounded(?) by what they have caught: men go to them of their own accord . . . . People say 'Do not walk here! Behold, it is a trap(?)!' Behold, people move like fish(?) . . .

Really, the desert is throughout the land, arable land is laid waste; a tribe from outside has come into Egypt . . . There are really no 'people' anywhere!

Really, gold, lapis, silver, malachite, carnelian, copper, diorite(?) and . . . adorn the necks of servant girls! Riches are throughout the land, but the ladies of the manor say 'Oh that we had something to eat!'

Really, . . . rich ladies, their bodies are ugly with rags, their hearts grieve(?) in greeting each other . . . .

Really, those who would have built tombs(?) are become peasants, and those who were in the god's boat are tied to the land. There are no sailings to Byblos these days. What shall we do for cedar for our mummies? Priests were buried with their products, and officials were embalmed with the oil thereof as far away as Keftiu; but it comes no longer. Gold is gone, and the raw material for every craft is used up, and the king's house L.P.H. is stripped bare. How important it (now) seems that oasis-people come bearing their festival goods! . . .

Really, laughter has perished and is no longer indulged in; crying it is that is throughout the land, mixed with lamentations.

Really, every corpse(?) is like him who still exists(?), and those who used to be 'people' have become alien and are cast aside.

Really, loss of hair is everyone's lot; one cannot tell a gentleman's son from him who has no distinguished father . . . .

Really, both prince and pauper say 'I want to die!' . . . .

Really, princes' offspring are dashed against walls, children of prayer are cast upon the high ground, and Khnum groans on account of his weariness.

Really, those who should be in the embalming house are cast on the high ground—that means difficulty for the embalmer[1]. . . .

Really, all maidservants are aggressive in their speech: when their mistresses speak it is irksome to the servants . . .

Really, princes hunger painfully, and the servants are served . . .

Really, paths are blocked and the road is guarded; people squat in the bushes until the night traveller comes along to seize his burden, and what he carries is stolen. He sniffs the blow of a stick and is killed wrongfully.

Really that has perished though seen only yesterday, and the land is left to its weakness, as when flax is pulled up. . . . Would that this meant the end of men, no conception, no birth; then the land would grow still from uproar, and there would be no strife! . . . .

Really, grain has perished on every hand! Clothing, spice and unguent are stripped away and everyone says 'There is nothing!' The storehouse is stripped bare, and its keeper is stretched out on the ground. . . .

Really, the holy castle, its documents are taken away; the place of secrets which used to be(?) is stripped bare!

Really, magic is laid bare! Go-incantations and Stay-incantations are ineffectual(?) because they are pronounced by men.

Really, offices are open and their accounts are taken away; people who were serfs have become lords of serfs. . . .

Really, as for the 'Scribes of the Mat' their ledgers are ignored, and Egypt's corn is a 'Come-and-get-it!'

Really, the laws of the castle are thrown outside; indeed, they are walked upon in public, and poor men tear them up in the streets!

Really, the poor man has achieved the status of an Ennead, and that rule of the cabinet is laid bare.

---

1. Casting the dead on high ground, i.e., the desert edge, was the way of disposing dishonorably of unwanted corpses. Once decomposition had set in, embalmers had a difficult task.

Really, the castle of the prince is a thoroughfare: poor men come and go in the Great Mansions.

Really, princes' children are thrown into the streets. I know it to be so, but the fool says: no. He who knows it not thinks things are fine. . . .

Behold, things have been done which have never happened for a long time: the king has been taken away by poor men.

Behold, he who was buried as a Falcon, now is on a common bier: what the pyramid concealed shall become empty.

Behold, it has come to the point where the land is deprived of the kingship by a few men who are ignorant of governance.

Behold, it has come to the point of people rebelling against the Uraeus, the champion(?) of Re, which deters the Two Lands. . . .

Behold, the *krht*-serpent is removed from her hole, and the secrets of the Kings of Upper and Lower Egypt are laid bare.

Behold, the royal residence fears from want, and all men provoke civil strife unopposed.

Behold, the land produces factions, and as for the brave man, the weak steals his goods. . . .

Behold, the possessors of embalming facilities are thrown down on the high ground, and he who never could acquire proper burial, now is owner of a treasury.

Behold, what has happened to people! He who never could build a shanty for himself now is owner of walls.

Behold, the councillors of the land are forcibly removed throughout the land, and there is general expulsion from the royal departments.

Behold, noble ladies are on rafts, and princes in the workhouse; but he who never slept indoors(?) is now owner of a bed.

Behold, the owner of property goes to bed thirsty, but he who had formerly to beg for scraps is now owner of overflowing vessels.

Behold, the owner of robes is in rags, but he who never wove for himself is now owner of linen.

Behold, he who never could construct ships is now owner of a fleet, while their former owner looks at them, but they are not his.

Behold, he who had no shade is now possessor of shade, while they who possessed shade now feel the full blast of the gale.

Behold, he who knew not the lyre now owns a harp; he who never sang for himself now extols the goddess Mert.

Behold, they who had offering stands of copper, not one of them has a vessel garlanded for him.

Behold, he who went to bed with no wife because of poverty finds riches; and he who never saw wealth is now loaded(?).

Behold, he who had no property is now possessor of wealth, and the prince praises him.

Behold, the indigent of the land are now become rich men, while the man of property is a pauper.

Behold, mat-makers(?) are become lords of butlers, and he who used to be a messenger now sends another.

Behold, he who had no loaf is owner of a barn, and his storehouse is stocked with another's property . . . .

Behold, the bosses of the land run away, they cannot govern because of want . . .

Behold, noble ladies are fallen into hunger, while the king's tenants are sated with what they have acquired.

Behold, every office is not functioning properly, like a herd running loose without a herdsman.

Behold, cattle stray away without anyone to round them up; everyone takes for himself and brands with his own name. . . .

Behold, he who had no team now owns a herd, he who could not find the wherewithal to do his own ploughing now owns cattle.

Behold, he who had no seed is now owner of a granary, and he who had to get himself a loan is now one who issues them.

Behold, he who had no neighbours, is now owner of serfs, he who was a prince now runs his own errands.

Behold, the magnates of the land are not reported to concerning the condition of the common people who have fallen into total loss.

Behold, no craftsmen labor; the land's enemies have impoverished its crafts. . . .

. . . . Behold, why does he seek to create men? The meek cannot be distinguished from the violent . . . They say he is the herdsman of everyone, and there is no evil in his heart. When his herd is thinned out, he spends the day rounding them up . . . Would that he had perceived their nature in the first generation, then he would have set obstacles, and stretched forth his arm, and destroyed

their seed and their heirs . . . Where is he today? Is he indeed
sleeping? Behold, his power is not seen. If we had been fed(?), I
should not have found thee, and I should not have been summoned
for nothing . . . . Creative Word, Intelligence and Truth are with
thee, but it is confusion that thou settest throughout the land and
the noise of battle: behold, people are attacking each other! People
conform to thy ordinance: if three men go along a road, they are
found to be two, for the greater number slays the lesser. Is the
herdsman, then, one that loves death? So thou hast replied: 'It is
because one loves and another hates, and that means the thinning
out of their beings everywhere.' So thou hast acted to bring this to
pass. Thou has spoken evil! . . . These many years have been spent
in strife. A man is killed on his own roof, while vigilant in his house
because of his boundary. Is he brave and does he look after himself? That means he will live. . . . Would that thou mightest taste
some of their misery! . . . (1)

Ancient Egypt also experienced destructive and costly wars
which accomplished little but a doubtful preservation of the
status quo. For a period of about thirty years (c. 1220–1190
B.C.) the country fought desperately to stave off invasion by
the Libyans and a horde of peoples from the northern coasts
of the Mediterranean. Though successful in beating back
armed invasion, the Egyptians in the two generations following the war suffered the grievous effects of their supreme effort. Prices of staples began to rise to a peak five times above
the former rate, workers refused to do their jobs, and tomb
robbery grew prevalent. It all sounds disturbingly like our
own postwar inflation, strikes and increased bank hold-ups.

The document translated below comes from the twenty-
ninth year of king Ramesses III (c. 1170 B.C.), and is now in
the Turin Museum. It is the official transcript, drawn up by
a government scribe, of one of the earliest workers' strikes on
record. The work-gang in question was the one which was
engaged in carving and decorating the king's rock-cut tomb
at Thebes, and the stoppage of the work at such a late point
in the reign—the king in fact died four years later—made the

administration rather anxious. Adding to their chagrin was the timing of the strike: on the eve of Ramesses' thirty-year jubilee, which was to take place at his residence Pi-Ramesses in the north of Egypt. To be noted especially is the lack of fear with which the workers walk off the job, and the lack of repression with which the administration handles the problem.

Regnal year 29, 2nd month of Spring, day 10: passing the five check-points of the royal tomb by the work-gang, saying 'We are hungry! Eighteen days have elapsed in the month!' And they sat down at the rear of the Mansion of Menkheperre. Came the scribe of the restricted royal tomb, the two foremen of the work-gang, the two deputies, and the two officers, and said 'Come inside.' But they took a great oath, saying 'You come out! We have things to say to Pharaoh, L.P.H.' Spending the day in this place; passing the night at the royal tomb (i.e. they returned to their quarters at nightfall).

Regnal year 29, 2nd month of Spring, day 12: arrival at the Mansion of Usermare Setepenre, passing the night in disorder(?) at its entry, and even entering inside it. The scribe Pentaweret, the chief of police, the two doorkeepers, the doorkeepers of the Keep of the royal tomb came, and the chief of police Montumose went to the city, saying 'I will fetch the mayor of the city,' . . . (now a new party of dignitaries, including priests, comes to see what is the matter, and the workers present their case to them). "And they said to them 'It's because of hunger and thirst that we have come to this! There's no clothing, no ointment, no fish, no vegetables! Send to Pharaoh, L.P.H., our good lord, about them, and send also to the vizier our superior, that sustenance may be provided for us.' And the rations for the first month of Spring were issued to them to-day.

Regnal year 29, 2nd. month of Spring, day 13: at the Keep of the royal tomb. What the chief of police Montumose said: 'See, I'll tell you my suggestion. Go up and gather your tools and lock your doors, and bring your wives and your children; and I will go ahead of you to the Mansion of Menmare, and I will let you stay there tomorrow.' Going to pass by the check-points at the rear of the town by the work-gang, although the three guards(?) had shouted aloud to them from the gate-house(?) of the town. Despatch of the two officers and the two deputies by Amun-nakht, scribe of the restricted royal tomb, to fetch them. Return by the officer Reshpetyef to tell us: 'thus spoke Qencna, son of Ruta, and Hay, son of Huy: "we will not come back! Tell that to your superiors! (now they were standing in front of their comrades). Really, it is not because of hunger that we have broken out. We have an important report to make: crimes are certainly being committed in this place of Pharaoh, L.P.H!" so they said.' When we went to hear their statements, they said to us 'that's truly what was said.'

Regnal year 29, 4th month of Spring, day 28: journey downstream by the vizier To, when he had come to take the gods of the Southland for the sed-festival. Came the chief of police Nebsumen, son of Pinehas, to tell the three guards of the work-gang who were standing at the Keep of the royal tomb: 'Thus says the vizier: "is there a reason for my not coming to you? It was not because there was nothing to bring you that I did not come. And when you say 'Don't take away our provisions!', am I, the vizier, one that gives only to take away? Have I not given what one in my station ought to give? If it ever happens that there is nothing at all in the granary, I will give you what I can find." ' And Hory, scribe of the royal tomb said to them: 'Half-rations are to be given you. I will distribute them to you myself.'

Regnal year 29, first month of Harvest, day 2: giving the two khar of emmer to the work-gang as rations of the first month of Harvest, by Amun-kha'u and Userhat. Said the foreman of the work-gang, Khonsu: 'see, what I'm telling you. Take the rations and go down to the harbour to the Keep; but let the "children of the vizier" tell it to him.' When the scribe Amun-nakhte had finished giving them the rations, they stationed themselves at the harbour, just as he had told them. And when they had passed one checkpoint the scribe Amun-nakhte came and said to them: 'Don't break out to the harbour, and I'll certainly give you two khar of emmer right away. But if you do go, I'll have you condemned in any court you may go to.' And he brought them up again.

Regnal year 29, first month of Harvest, day 13: breaking through the check-points by the work-gang with the words: 'We are hungry!' Squatting at the rear of the Mansion of Baenre Meryamun. They called to the mayor of the city who was passing by, and he sent them the gardener of the superintendent of cattle, Meniunofer, to tell them: 'Look! I give you this fifty *khar* of emmer as sustenance until Pharaoh, L.P.H. gives you your rations.'

Regnal year 29, first month of Harvest, day 16: what the workman Pen'anukis said to the scribe Amun-nakhte and the foreman Khonsu: 'You are my superiors, and you are the administrators of the royal tomb. Now Pharaoh, L.P.H., my good lord, made me take an oath that I would not hear anything or see any crimes in these great and deep places and conceal them. Now Userhat and Pentaweret have stripped off stone from above the tomb of Osiris king Usermare Setepenre, L.P.H., the great god. And he took a bull branded with the brand of the Mansion of Usermare Setepenre, and it (now) stands in his barn. And he raped three married women, the citizeness Menat who is married to Qnena, the citizeness Tayuna who is married to Nakhtamun, and the citizeness Tawerthotpety who is married to Pentaweret . . . (2)

The practice of relying on informers was probably as unreliable in Egypt of the 12th Century B.C. as it was later to be in Rome of the First Century A.D., or even in the drug culture of the 20th Century A.D. But whether or not Userhat and Pentaweret were guilty in reality, the general picture vouchsafed by the foregoing account reflects what the ancient Egyptian feared most: stasis[2] and revolution. Ironically, from the lips of Ramesses III himself, the very king against whose administration these strikes were aimed, comes perhaps the pithiest sketch of what in ancient Egypt revolution really meant. Ramesses here describes the condition of the country immediately before his father's accession; and in typical Egyptian fashion blame is laid on the meddling of foreigners and the abandonment of the gods:

Said Usermare Meriamun, L.P.H., the great god, to the princes and commanders of the land, the army, the cavalry, the Sherdenmercenaries, the numerous batallions, and all the citizens of the land of Egypt: 'Hear ye, and I will inform you of my good works

2. *Stasis* is used here as it was in classical Greek politics: party-fighting or factionalism.

which I wrought, when I was the king of the people. The land of
Egypt had been thrown into disorder, and every man was a law
unto himself, for they had no leader. For many years formerly until
a certain period the land of Egypt had princes and reeves who slew
one another, both high and low. The period following this con-
sisted of empty years, when a Syrian who was with them made himself prince, and he put the entire land to work for him. People
were slaying each other, and their goods were stolen; and gods were
treated just like men, and no offerings were presented in the temples . . .' (3)

4

"Revered Before His Lord"

The Egyptian Autobiography

1. THE DECEASED REQUESTS

The most common wish of the blessed departed in Ancient Egypt was for good burial, perpetual offerings of foodstuffs for the spirit, and successful attainment of heaven ("the West"). Offerings were made at the tomb on feast days by relatives of the dead man, and by the lector priest hired for the job before the tomb-owner's death. But even the recitation of a set formula was deemed sufficient to make offerings in royal chapels and the temples of the gods available by magical means to the deceased, after the divine residents of those shrines had had their fill of them. These oral, "invocation offerings" are couched in the form of an incantation beginning "An Offering which the king gives," and even passers-by are coaxed and

cajoled by inscriptions on the lintel and façade of the tomb
to pronounce the spell on the dead man's behalf.

An offering which the king gives and an offering which Anubis
gives, He-who-is-upon-his-hill, Foremost of the god's-booth, He-who-
is-in-the-Sepulchre, Lord of the Elevated Ground, that he (the tomb
owner) may be buried in the necropolis of the Western Desert in
very good old age as one revered by the Great God. . . .
   An offering which the king gives, and an offering which Osiris
Lord of Busiris gives that he (the tomb owner) may journey in
peace upon the elevated roads of the West whereon the revered
ones journey; and that he may mount up to god, the Lord of
Heaven, as one revered by the Great God, namely the count and
chamberlain, 'Herdsman of Nekhen,' chief Nekhbite, sole companion, lector priest, revered by Osiris, Hor-khuef. (1)
   O ye who are upon earth—scribes, lector-priests, ordinary priests,
mortuary priests—who may see this monument, my likeness, my
'heir' upon earth, my memorial in the necropolis! Your gods shall
favour and love you, you shall be rejuvenated in life and shall pass
on your offices to your children, if ye say 'An offering which the
king gives to Amunre and Atum' for the spirit of the mayor and
vizier User, deceased. . . . This is not something that makes one
weary. I am wont to bestow favour on him who is in my shadow,
and one who pronounces my name is esteemed thereby. If ye do
this, it will go well with you, you shall prosper and be free from
harm. Do not shut your ears to what I say, for I am an official who
is used to being obeyed! (2)
   An offering which the king gives to Osiris, Lord of Busiris, and
Khentiamentiu Lord of Abydos, in all his cult seats, that invocation offerings may proceed of a thousand of bread and beer, a
thousand of beef and fowl, a thousand of various fine and pure
things . . . the provisions of the Lord of Abydos, after his spirit
is satisfied therewith, for the revered one, the seal-bearer of the
king of Lower Egypt, the general of the army of the entire land,
Antef, deceased. (3)
   Ye shall offer me of that which is in your hands. But if there is

nothing in your hand, you shall say orally 'A thousand of bread, beer, beef, fowl, etc. . . . to the spirit of . . .' (4)

The offering-formula (pronounced audibly) is indeed no outlay of your own wealth, but simply breath of the mouth, of advantage to the noble; for a good deed is more advantageous to him who does it than to him for whom it is done. (5)

2. THE DECEASED THREATENS

The closest approach to the proverbial "curse" with which the ancient Egyptians are widely believed to have cursed would-be violators of their tombs is exemplified in the following threats to any who may seek to harm the tomb-owner's descendants or his monuments.

The eldest of the house, Meny, says: 'may a crocodile be against him on the water, and a snake against him on land, (viz. against) any who may do anything to this inscription; for I have never done anything to him! God it is that shall judge him!' (1)

I came forth from my town, and descended from my township. I was one that spoke what is good, and repeated what is good. As for any man who may do anything to my children, I shall be judged with him by the great god in the place where this sort of thing is judged. (2)

Graffito with figure of the writer, the seal-bearer of the king of Lower Egypt Amenemhet, recording quarry-work done in the 31st year of Senwosret I (c. 1940 B.C.): As for any craftsman, or any traveller, or any people who shall raise their hand to this representation (i.e. the graffito), Anty it is that shall favour him. But as for him who shall destroy my name from this representation, the gods of the Hermopolite township shall remove his children from his office after his death! (3)

3. THE DECEASED NARRATES

After the mortuary prayer, titles and name, in the normal sequence of elements in a funerary text, comes the narration in direct speech of the dead man's virtues and distinctions, the whole introduced by the formula "he says." While relatively rare until the last two centuries of the Old Kingdom, this part of the customary inscription was to blossom forth after the close of the Pyramid Age into a more or less stereotyped biographical sketch. The intent of the speaker was, of course, to win the approbation of posterity; but to us moderns his narrative often proves to be a valuable source of historical and sociological information.

The Old Kingdom produced a class of extremely capable and diligent civil servants, often of relatively low estate. Selected at the behest of the king and his high ministers, and trained at the Memphite court, these energetic bureaucrats are found throughout the kingdom and the adjacent lands busily engaged in leading mining or quarrying expeditions, directing punitive attacks on obstinate tribes, or acquiring commodities through trade or exaction for the king's treasury. One can sense in the description of the career of a man like Weny a good deal of enthusiasm for the tasks he was assigned, and pride in the success he achieved in carrying them out. But, like a good servant of the divine king, the "good god," he is careful to point out the perspicacity of the king in recognizing his ability, and to ascribe the power to accomplish great things to the king alone.

Count, Governor of Upper Egypt, He-Who-Is-In-The-Chamber, Herdsman of Nekhen, Chief of Nekheb, courtier, revered before Osiris First-of-Westerners, Weny. He says:

'I was a fillet-wearing child during the time of the Majesty of Tety, when my office was that of overseer of the work-house, and I functioned as Sub-director of Palace market-gardeners. While(?) I was . . . . lector-priest and Eldest of the Ornamented Facade during the time of the Majesty of Pepy (I), his Majesty put me in the office of courtier-sub-director of priests of his pyramid-city, though my office had been only that of . . . . His Majesty then made me Judge-attached-to-Nekhen, since he trusted me more than any other servant of his. I used to hear cases alone with the Chancellor, Judge, and Vizier in all private matters that came up(?) sealed in the name of the king, or of the king's harim, or of the Six Great Courts of Justice; for His Majesty trusted me more than any official of his, any noble of his, or any servant of his. I requested the Majesty of my lord that a limestone coffin be brought for me from Turah. His Majesty had a God's-seal-bearer take ship with a captain's crew which was under his charge to bring this coffin from Turah for me. It came accompanying him in a great transport boat belonging to the king's residence, along with its portucullis(?), a false door with emplacement(?), two base(?) blocks and one libation stone. Never had the like been done for any servant!

Then I proved capable in His Majesty's opinion, then I proved congenial in His Majesty's opinion, then His Majesty put trust in me; and while my office was only that of Judge-attached-to-Nekhen His Majesty made me courtier-overseer of Palace market-gardeners. I replaced four overseers of Palace-gardeners who had formerly been there (i.e. in the office I now occupied alone). I acted in conformity with what His Majesty likes, in doing personal service, on royal progresses, and in performing court functions. I did everything so well that His Majesty praised me for it beyond anything.

When legal proceedings were initiated in camera in the royal harim against the Great King's-Wife . . . His Majesty had me go in to hear the case alone. There was no Chancellor Judge and Vizier there, nor any official save me alone, for I was capable, for I was congenial in His Majesty's opinion, for His Majesty trusted me. It was I that put it in writing all by myself together with one Judge-attached-to-Nekhen, although my office was only that of overseer of Palace market-gardeners. Never before had one of my rank heard a case of the royal harim in camera; but His Majesty allowed me to hear the case, because I was more capable in His Majesty's opinion than any official of his, than any noble of his, or than any servant of his.

When His Majesty would punish the Asiatics who are over the sand His Majesty made an army of many tens of thousands recruited from all Upper Egypt from Elephantine in the south to the Aphroditopolite nome in the north, and from Lower Egypt throughout the entire two administrative districts, and from the keeps(?) and from the environs(?) of the keeps(?), from the southerners of

Irchet, Madja, Wawat and Kaaw, and from those of the land of
Tjemeh. His Majesty sent me in command of this army, while the
counts, seal-bearers of the king of Lower Egypt, and the courtiers of
the Great Palace, and while the chiefs, the palace-rulers of Upper
and Lower Egypt, the courtier-superintendents of mercenaries, the
bishops of Upper and Lower Egypt, and the overseers of departments
were each in charge of the troops of the estates and towns of Upper
and Lower Egypt which they governed, as well as the southerners of
these foreign lands. It was I that took charge of them, although my
office was only that of overseer of Palace market-gardeners, because of
the exactitude with which I discharged my office. And the result was
that nobody quarreled with his fellow, nobody stole a loaf or a pair
of sandals from a traveller, nobody seized a garment from any town,
and nobody seized a goat from any persons. I led them by way of
the "Northern Fort(?)," through(?) the "Gate of Imhotpe," in(?) the
March of Horus Lord of Truth. . . . Each of these troops was drawn
up for my inspection although never had a drawing up for inspection been done for any servant.

This army returned in peace, having hacked up the land of them
who are across the sand!

This army returned in peace, having pulverized the land of them
who are across the sand!

This army returned in peace, having razed its fortified cities!

This army returned in peace, having cut down its fig-trees and
vines!

This army returned in peace, having set all its dwellings(?) on
fire!

This army returned in peace, having slain the enemy troops that
were in it by the many tens of thousands!

This army returned in peace, having brought off very many of
the enemy troops that were in it as prisoners!

And His Majesty praised me for it beyond anything! His Majesty
sent me to lead this army on five occasions, to smite the land of
those who are over the sand, every time they rebelled, with these
troops. I did it so well that His Majesty praised me for it beyond
anything. Then it was reported that there were trouble-makers
among these foreigners in the land of "Gazelle-nose(?)", and so I
crossed the sea in transport ships with these troops, and put to shore

behind the height of the ridge on the north of the land of those across the sand. With a full half(?) of these troops afar off (i.e. out of the battle?) I returned, having captured them all; and the trouble-makers among them were slain.

When I served as Palace-intendant bearing the sandals, the king of Upper and Lower Egypt, Merenre, my lord living forever, appointed me count-governor of Upper Egypt from Elephantine in the south to the Aphroditopolite nome in the north, because I was capable in His Majesty's opinion, because I was congenial in His Majesty's opinion, and because His Majesty put his trust in me. And when I occupied the post of intendant bearing the sandals, His Majesty praised me for the vigilance with which I exercised the personal service in court functions, more than any official of his, more than any noble of his, more than any servant of his. Never before had this office been filled by any mere servant. I exercised the governorship of Upper Egypt commendably for him, and the result was that nobody quarreled with his fellow. I performed every task and made assessment on two occasions of all the goods assessed for the Residence in this Upper Egypt, as well as on two occasions all the corvée assessed for the residence in this Upper Egypt. I functioned in the office which is responsible for everything in this Upper Egypt. Never before had anything like this been done in this Upper Egypt, and I performed everything so well that His Majesty praised me for it.

His Majesty despatched me to Ibhat to fetch a sarcophagus "a chest of the living," along with its lid and a pyramidion—a precious and valuable object—for the pyramid called "Merenre-Shines-and-is-Beautiful," the Mistress. His Majesty despatched me to Elephantine to fetch a false door with its libation stone of granite, and granite portcullises and settings(?), and to fetch the granite doors and libation stones of the Upper Shrine of the pyramid "Merenre-Shines-and-is-Beautiful," the Mistress. They sailed downstream with me to the Pyramid "Merenre-Shines-and-is-Beautiful" in six barges, three cargo boats and three "Eight"-boats—all in one expedition! Never in the time of any of the former kings had Ibhat and Elephantine been visited on a single expedition. And everything His Majesty had commanded was brought to completion through my agency, exactly as His Majesty had commanded.

His Majesty despatched me to Hatnub to fetch a great offering table of Hatnub alabaster. I built a barge for it of acacia wood, 60 cubits long and 30 cubits wide, caulked (i.e. completed) in 17 days in the third month of *shomu*. I sent this offering table off to him in 17 days, quarried from Hatnub and shipped downstream in this barge. And although the water did not cover the sandbanks, it docked safely at the pyramid "Merenre-Shines-and-is-Beautiful." All this happened through my agency according to the command issued by the Majesty of my lord.

His Majesty dispatched me to cut 5 canals in Upper Egypt and to make three barges and 4 cargo boats of acacia wood of Wawat; and the foreign chiefs of Irtjet, Wawat, Yam, and Madja hauled the wood for it. I did it all in one year, and when the waters rose, they were despatched loaded very heavily with granite for the Pyramid "Merenre-Shines-and-is-Beautiful." Indeed I had saved time for the Palace by each of these five canals, because the power of the king of Upper and Lower Egypt, Merenre, living for ever, was rarer(?), mightier and loftier than all the gods, and because in fact everything happened according to the command issued by his *ku*.

I am indeed one beloved of his father, praised of his mother, and pleasing to his brethren, the true count-governor of Upper Egypt, revered before Osiris, Weny. (1)

4. THE DECEASED BOASTS

At the close of the Sixth Dynasty, shortly after 2200 B.C., the theocratic state of the aloof god-king suffered a breakdown, and the central authority of the Residence at Memphis existed in name only. The administrative framework wherein the Egyptians had lived and enjoyed security was no more. Where could people turn for protection and leadership now? In the absence of any central, unifying force of royal authorship, the man who could command a gang of armed men became the only sure agent of law and order. People flocked about such a man in desperation, and supported him literally for their lives. The mortuary texts of such squires of the local manor, whether on slab stelae or in the crude, rock-cut tombs they have left behind, are often richer in biographical material than the wordy texts of their Old Kingdom forebears. Whereas the latter boasted of their rank and relation to the king, the new breed of provincial count is aware—and proud—of his real independence and self-reliance. He boasts of deeds, not titles, and rarely mentions the king. He stresses that his property is his own, not the bequest of an outsider; and he presents himself as a simple, but able, man, the guarantor of law and order.

An offering that the king gives . . . to the count, seal-bearer of the king of Lower Egypt, courtier-lector, the revered Yenedy. He says: 'I am a commoner who is good at fighting, a friend of outdoorsmen(?). I am one loved of his father, praised of his mother, beloved by his brethren, pleasant to his family and children. I was elevated from the back of my father's house through the might of Anhur, and I ruled Thinis because of my character(?) and for the sake of getting things done properly. I am one who speaks with his mouth and acts with his arm. There is no man who speaks against the revered Yenedy.' (1)
. . . I acquired people, cattle, flocks, asses, grain, clothing, unguent(?); I placed a ship on the water, trees in the field(?). What I did was by my own strength. (2)

Often a man will boast, under the new dispensation, of his relationship to a provincial official in much the same terms as formerly under the Old Kingdom one would have spoken of one's ties to the king.

Regnal years 7 of the count, controller of the two thrones, bishop, nomarch of the Hermopolite township, king's acquaintance, pre-eminent in Upper Egypt, Nehri born of Kemy, living forever! The superintendent of the lake, Sobekemhat, says: 'Even when I was a child I was a courtier and a man of the audience chamber without peer. . . . Greater was the favour for me than that for a son, through the agency of my lord; and that's common knowledge. I am speaking the truth! But even when I was in such favour, I bore it patiently: I did not rob another man of his property, I did not divest a poor man of his plot, there was no complaint about me from anyone. . . . I functioned as superintendent of the lake during the time of the count Nehri, life! prosperity! health! Greater was the favour for me through his agency than that for a son or a brother. . . . I did service under him in his house, nor was I allowed to see the shade of another place except when he sent me to Hatnub to fetch him alabaster blocks of the sort destined for the king's house. A full(?) writing was made for me personally, as for a son or a brother, concerning(?) my trip hither; for indeed I performed the service in this highland cooly and calmly . . . . and I departed hence with happy heart, having accomplished what I came for. I have surpassed all men! As Nehri born of Kemy lives for me, I am speaking the truth! Now as for any traveller who shall raise his hand in respect to this representation (i.e. the picture of Sobekemhat which accompanies the text), he shall reach home safely having accomplished what he went for. (3)

The prevalence of disorder and intestine feuds in the period following the demise of the Old Kingdom created a class of nomarchs, steeled to fighting and inured to brutality. Perhaps the best example of this type of militaristic braggart is Ankhtify-nakht of Mo'alla, the nomarch of the third Upper Egyptian township, who lived during the first half of the Twentysecond Century B.C. The "Band of Hefat" which he elsewhere refers to was, in fact, his private army, recruited from his home township. The reasons given for his meddling in his neighbours' affairs sound surprisingly modern: he was forced to intervene in order to restore law and order, or he was requested by beleaguered governments to supply military aid, or—and admittedly this is a little passé—God told him to step in!

Horus brought me to the Edfu-nome (the second Upper Egyptian nome) for its own life, prosperity and health. Now Horus was desirous that I should re-establish it, since he brought me to it to re-establish it. I found the domain of Khuu under water like a swamp(?), neglected by its keeper, badly managed under the administration of a wretch. I caused a man to embrace the one who had slain his father or slain his brother, in order to re-establish order in the nome of Edfu. How happy the day when prosperity was found in this nome! (4)

The military governor of Ermant came to say: 'see now, O brave male! Come north to the fortresses of Ermant!' I went north on the west of Ermant (5) and I found that the entire nomes of Thebes and Coptos were besieging(?) the fortress of Ermant. . . . Then (my arms) waxed strong against them like a harpoon(?) lodged in the nose of a fleeing hippopotamus.

I am the front of men and the rear of men, one who finds the solution when in need of it(?), at the head of the land, because of forthright plans(?); one controlled of speech with his wits about him . . .

A man like me has never appeared, nor will he appear, has never been born nor will he be born. I have gone beyond what my forebears did, and my successors will not surpass me in anything I have done for a million years."

5

"... in the Stories of Those Who Were Aforetime"

Egyptian Narratives

Ancient Egypt has been claimed to be the home of the Short Story. Facile as such a statement seems to be, it does indicate the fact of Egypt's primacy in the ancient world as the seat of a strong and creative narrative tradition. Not infrequently in the selections translated below, plot and incidental motif will occur which are more familiar to us in later European folklore, which borrowed them, often indirectly, from their Egyptian source.

We moderns apply the adjective "literary" to such a tradition; but this anachronism simply betrays how thoroughly the Gutenberg revolution has affected us. For in a society where the majority of the population is illiterate there is no point to committing compositions to writing; nor will composers of narrative feel much compunction to create through the medium of writing. In the stories translated in the next two chapters we must see a reflection of what the Egyptians loosely called *sdd*, "narrative," "something passed on by the spoken word," which was at least communicated, if not originally composed, orally and designed for a live audience. This is not to deny the existence of a strong scribal tradition side by side with the oral, which was influenced strongly by it. In fact, *The Trial of Horus and Seth*, translated in the next chapter, is probably, in the form in which it occurs in the Chester Beatty Papyrus, a written work rather than a copy of an oral delivery. But throughout all Egyptian history, the phenomenon of a gifted orator delivering himself to an audience for their entertainment represents the basic mode of narrative composition.

THE TALE OF THE SHIPWRECKED SAILOR

This fantastic yarn, written on a papyrus of the 19th century B.C. now in Leningrad, is a prototype of the kind of story most familiar to us from the Sindbad cycle. The speaker, an unnamed retainer, is trying to cheer up the commander of an expedition returning from Nubia. Apparently things have not gone well, and the commander fears what the king will say. The last line shows that the commander has not been encouraged by the retainer's rather naive narrative. Like the *Doomed Prince* and the *Tale of Two Brothers* translated below, the *Shipwrecked Sailor* belongs to a category of folktale which makes little or no use of proper names and is not dated to a particular point in time.

Said the worthy retainer: 'Rest thy heart, O commander! See, we have reached home! The mallet has been taken in hand, and the mooring post fixed; the prow-rope has been thrown on shore, and they are shouting for joy and thanking god, and everyone is embracing his companion. (For) our crew has returned safe, and our expedition has suffered no loss. We have reached the limit of

Wawat, and have passed Senmet! We have returned in peace and reached our land!

Listen to me, commander! I am not an excessive person. Wash thyself and put water on thy hands; so thou shalt answer when thou art addressed and speak to the king with thy wits about thee, and answer without hesitation. A man's speech it is that saves him, his words it is that make people favorably disposed towards him. Act thou in thy proper frame of mind. Speaking to thee is tiresome, so I shall tell thee something similar which happened to me myself:

I went to the "Mine-land" of the Sovereign, and I embarked on the sea in a ship 120 cubits long and 40 cubits wide, with a crew of 120 on board, drawn from the best sailors in Egypt. No matter where they looked, up or down, their hearts were as imperturbable as those of lions; they could predict a storm before it came, or a tempest before it happened. A storm blew up while we were on the sea, before we could get to land. The wind rose to double its normal strength, and with it came waves 8 cubits high which the mast broke for me. Then the ship sank and none of those who were in her survived. Then I was deposited upon an island by a wave of the sea.

I spent three days by myself, my heart my sole companion, sleeping in a bower of wood, for I sought out the shade. Then I got up to find out what I could put in my mouth, and I discovered figs and grapes as well as all sorts of good vegetables. There were sycamore figs there, and notched figs, and cucumbers, as though they had been cultivated; fish were there, and fowl, and there was nothing which was not in it (i.e. the island). Then I feasted myself, and had even to leave some on the ground, for I had too much to carry. I took out a fire-drill, made a fire, and offered a holocaust to the gods.

Then I heard a thunderous noise, which I took to be a wave of the sea. Trees were cracking, the earth was shaking. When I uncovered my face I found it was a snake that was coming, 30 cubits in length, with a beard longer than two cubits. His body was overlaid with gold, his brows were of real lapis, and his foreparts stood upright. And he opened his mouth to me—now I was on my belly before him—and he said to me: "Who brought you? Who brought

you, little one? Who brought you? If you delay in telling me who
brought you to this island, I shall let you know what it's like to be
burnt to a crisp, having become something which never was seen!"
Then I answered him: "Though thou speakest to me, I do not
understand it; though I am before thee, I do not know myself."
Then he put me in his mouth and took me to his place of abode,
and put me down without hurting me, in a safe condition, without
roughly handling me.

Then he opened his mouth to me, while I was on my belly before him, and he said to me: "Who brought you? Who brought you,
little one? Who brought you to this island of the sea whose sides
are water?" Then I answered him, with my arms bent respectfully
before him, and I said to him: "It happened that I embarked for
the 'Mine-land' on the Sovereign's mission in a ship 120 cubits long
and 40 cubits wide, with a crew of 120 on board, drawn from the
best sailors in Egypt. No matter where they looked, up or down,
their hearts were as imperturbable as those of lions; they could
predict a storm before it came, or a tempest before it happened.
Everyone of them was imperturbable, with an arm stronger than
his companion's—there was no fool among them. A storm blew up
while we were on the sea, before we could get to land. The wind
rose to double its normal strength, and with it came waves 8 cubits
high, which the mast broke for me. Then the ship sank, and none
of those who were in her survived, except me—and here I am beside thee! Then I was brought to this island by a wave of the sea."

Said he to me: "do not fear, little one! Let not your face go pale,
now that you have reached me. Behold, god it is that has let you
live, that has brought you to this 'Island of the *Ku*'. There is nothing which is not in it, it is filled with every good thing. Behold, you
shall spend month after month until you have completed four
months on this island, and a ship will come from home, with sailors
in it whom you know. You shall go home with them, and die in
your city.

How happy is one who can relate what he has experienced after
the painful event has passed! Let me tell you something which
happened on this island when I lived here with my brothers and
the children all together. We totalled 75 snakes, my offspring and
my brothers; I will not mention to you the little daughter whom

I got through prayer. Then a star fell, and they perished in the fire from it. It happened when I was not with them, they burned up while I was not in their midst. Then I died for them(?), for I found them a single heap of corpses. If you are brave and your heart stout, put your children in your embrace, kiss your wife, look upon your house: that is better than anything else. When you reach home, stay there with your brothers!"

Now I, being stretched flat upon my belly, touched the earth before him, and I said to him: "I shall relate thy might to the Sovereign, I shall acquaint him with thy greatness! I shall have sent thee ladanum[1](?), festival oil, incense, spice, and incense of the temples wherewith the gods are propitiated. I shall tell what has happened, paying close attention to what I have seen of thy(!) might, and they will thank god for you in the City, in the presence of the council of the entire land. I shall sacrifice cattle to thee in a holocaust, and I will wring the necks of fowl for thee. I shall have ships sent thee laden with all the luxuries of the land of Egypt, as they do for a god whom people love in a far-off land which people do not know."

Then he laughed at me, because what I had said seemed foolish to him, and he said to me: "you do not have much myrrh, that you should act like the owner of incense! But I am the ruler of Pwenet! Myrrh belongs to me, and that festival oil which you talked of bringing, it's a major product of this island! It will happen that when you remove yourself from this place, you will never again see this island, for it shall have turned into waves."

Then came that ship as he had earlier predicted. Then I went and climbed a high tree, and recognized those who were in it; and I went to inform him, but I found that he knew it already.

Then he said to me: "Safe journey, little one! Safe journey to your house! Look upon your children, and put my good reputation in your city. Behold, it is my due from you." Then I threw myself on my belly, my arms bent before him; and he presented me with a cargo of myrrh, festival oil, frankincense(?), spice, gum(?), . . . , eye-paint, giraffe-tails, great lumps of incense, elephant tusks, dogs, apes, monkeys, and all fine products; and I loaded it into this ship. It happened that, when I threw myself on my belly to thank god

1. A variant of *labdanum*, a resin used in perfumery.

for him, he said to me: "Behold, you shall reach home in two months. Fill your embrace with your children, prosper you at home, and have a proper burial there!"

Then I went down to the shore near this ship, and I called out to the expedition which was on board; and on the shore I gave praise to the lord of this island, and those who were on board did the same.

So we journeyed northward to the residence of the Sovereign, and we arrived home in two months just as he had said. Then I went in unto the Sovereign, and presented him with this cargo which I had brought from the island, and he thanked god for me before the council of the entire land. I was promoted to the office of retainer, and endowed with 200 domestics. Look at me, now that I have reached home, now that I have seen what I experienced! Listen to my words! Behold, it is good for people to listen!'

Then he (i.e. the commander) said to me: 'Don't act too clever, my friend. Is water indeed given to a fowl at daybreak on the morning when it is to be slaughtered?'

(Colophon) Reproduced from beginning to end, as it was found in writing by the able-fingered scribe, Ameny's son, Amen-o, L.P.H." (1)

THE TALE OF APOPHIS AND SEQNENRE

This free-wheeling yarn, unfortunately incomplete, is preserved on a papyrus of the late 13th century B.C. now in the British Museum. It purports to account for the outbreak of the war of liberation of the 16th century B.C. in which the Hyksos conquerors were expelled from Egypt, by putting it down to the provocation of the Hyksos ruler, Apophis, in his attempt to promulgate the worship of his pet god, Seth. Although personal names and toponyms are historical, and the atmosphere of antipathy is authentic, no reliance should be placed in the story as an accurate reflection of the real causes of the war. The fantastic charge of Apophis, viz. that he cannot sleep because of the bellowing of the hippopotami at Thebes hundreds of miles away, belongs in the realm of folklore, and

partakes of the well-known motif in which two hostile opponents, instead of going to war, engage in a battle of wits involving wildly exaggerated charge and counter-charge. If the
tale were complete, we should probably see that Seqnenre won
the day, after an exchange of insulting messages, by posing a
demand or a riddle which Apophis could not respond to.

It happened once that the land of Egypt was afflicted by plague,
and there was no lord, L.P.H., or king of the hour. But it happened
that, while king Seqenenre L.P.H. acted as ruler L.P.H. of the
Southern City, plague was in the city of Re(?), and prince Apophis
L.P.H. was in Avaris. He had put the entire land under taxation,
the North(?) as well, yielding all the fine products of the Delta.

Then king Apophis made Seth his lord, nor did he serve any
other god in the entire land except Seth; and he built a temple of
fine and enduring work beside the 'House of king Apophis L.P.H.,
and there he appeared every day to make the daily sacrifice to
Seth, while the courtiers of the palace L.P.H. carried garlands, exactly as it is done in the temple of Re-harakhty. Now king Apophis
L.P.H. wished to send insulting messages to king Seqenenre L.P.H.
the Prince of the Southern City.

Now after many days had passed, king Apophis L.P.H. summoned
the princes(?) and the courtiers of his palace(?) and he said to them
. . ." (The king's speech is almost entirely lost in a lacuna).

"Then said the scribes, the wise-men . . . : 'O Sovereign L.P.H.
our lord! Say thus: "Do away(?) with the hippopotamus pool which
is on the east of the city, for they prevent us sleeping day and night,
their noise being in the ears of our city . . ."

Now after many days had passed king Apophis L.P.H. sent to the
prince of the Southern City the verbal message his scribes and wise
men had suggested to him. When the messenger of king Apophis
L.P.H. arrived at the Southern City, he was taken into the presence
of the prince of the Southern City. Then they said to the messenger
of king Apophis L.P.H: 'Why have you been sent to the Southern
City? Why have you made this journey?' Then the messenger said
to him: 'King Apophis L.P.H. sends to you, saying, "Do away(?)
with the hippopotamus pool which is on the east side of the city,

for they prevent me sleeping day and night," their noise being in the ears of his city.'

Then the prince of the Southern City was silent for a long time; and he found himself unable to answer the messenger of king Apophis L.P.H. Then the prince of the Southern City said to him: 'Wherein(?) has your master L.P.H. heard tell of the hippopotamus pool which is on the east of the Southern City?' Then the messenger said to him: '———— the things concerning which he sent me.'

Then the prince of the Southern City had fine provisions assigned to the messenger of king Apophis L.P.H. of meat and cakes . . . . . and the prince of the Southern City said to him: 'Say to your master, "Whatever you say to me I will do it!" Tell him that . . . .' Then the messenger of king Apophis betook himself to journey to the place where his master L.P.H. was. Thereupon the prince of the Southern City summoned his magnates and all the soldiers and army officers, and he repeated to them every matter that king Apophis L.P.H. had sent to him about. But they were silent to a man for a long time; they could answer him neither good nor ill. Then king Apophis L.P.H. sent to the prince of the Southern City again(?), saying . . . (The rest is lost). (2)

THE STORY OF THE DOOMED PRINCE

Pre-occupation with one's destiny, and whether one can in any way control it, is not typical of Egyptian speculative thought. Nevertheless hemerologies do sometimes show an interest in how from the day or circumstances of a man's birth his ultimate fate may be descried. The tale translated below adopts as its theme an individual's vicissitudes, who, doomed at birth to die in a certain manner, attempts to ward off his fate. Although the papyrus, dated around 1300 B.C. and now in the British Museum, breaks off before the end of the story, depriving us of certitude regarding the author's complete view of life, it seems more likely that the piece had a "happy ending" than that it made its hero succumb to his fate.

Now they say there was once a king to whom no male child had been born. His Majesty prayed for a boy from the gods of his time, and they decreed that one should be born to him; and he slept at night with his wife, and she arose(?) pregnant. She completed her months of confinement and then a male child was born. Up came the 'Hathors' to set him a fate, and they said: 'He shall die by a crocodile, a snake, or a dog.' Thereupon, when the people who attended the child heard, they repeated it to His Majesty L.P.H. Then His Majesty's heart was exceedingly sad, and His Majesty had built for him a house of stone upon the highlands, and it was equipped with people and every good thing of the king's house L.P.H; and the child did not go forth from it.

Now after the child had grown he climbed up to his roof, and saw a dog following behind a man who was coming along the road. And he said to his servant who was at his side: 'What's that going behind the grown-up who is coming along the road?' And he said to him: 'It's a dog.' And the child said to him: 'Get me one just like it!' Then the Servant went and told His Majesty L.P.H., and His Majesty L.P.H. said: 'Have a little puppy taken to him, and his heart will not be sad.' So they took him a dog.

Now after some time had passed, and the lad had grown to be an adult, he sent to his father saying: 'What is the purpose of my sitting here? For see! I am doomed to the fates. Let me be free that I may do as I please, and let God do as he wishes!' Then a chariot was harnessed for him, equipped with various weapons of war, and a servant(?) was given to him(?) as retainer; and he was rowed across to the eastern cliffs, and they said to him: 'so go where you please,' and his dog was with him. And he went north as he pleased over the desert, his sustenance being the best of the desert game. Came he then to the Chief of Naharin's place. Now only a daughter had been born to the Chief of Naharin, and a house had been built for her with a window 70 cubits above the ground (c. 116 feet); and he had had brought all the sons of all the chiefs of the land of Syria, and had said to them: 'He who reaches my daughter's window shall have her to wife.'

Now after many days had passed, they being occupied in their normal daily round, the lad did pass by them. Then they took the lad to their house and washed him, and they gave fodder to his horses, and they treated the lad very well; and they anointed him and bandaged his feet, and they gave his retainer bread. And they said to him by way of conversation: 'Where do you come from, fine fellow?' And he said to them: 'I am the son of an officer of the land of Egypt. My mother died and my father took a second wife, and she began to hate me, so I have run away from her.' And they embraced him and kissed him all over.

Now after many days had passed, he said to the boys: 'What are you doing?' And they said to him: 'For . . . months until now we have been here, spending time jumping, and the one who shall reach the window of the Chief of Naharin's daughter, he will give her to him to wife.' And he said to them: 'Oh that I were not foot-sore(?), (or) I would come to jump with you.' And they went to jump, as was their daily custom, while the lad stood afar off watching; and the Chief of Naharin's daughter was looking at him.

Now sometime later the lad came to jump with the chiefs' boys, and he jumped and reached the window of the Chief of Naharin's daughter, and she kissed him and embraced him all over. Then they went to inform her father, and they said to him: 'Someone has reached your daughter's window!' Then the chief enquired saying: 'The son of which chief?' And they said to him: 'The son of an officer who has run away out of the land of Egypt from his stepmother.' Then the Chief of Naharin was exceedingly angry and said: 'Shall I give my daughter to an Egyptian run-away? Let him go back!' And they went and said to him: 'So go back to the place where you came from.' But the girl seized him and swore by god: 'As Re-harakhty endures! If they take him away from me I shall not eat, I shall not drink, I shall die at once!' Then the messenger went to make a full report of what she said to her father; and her father sent people to slay him on the spot. But the girl said: 'As Re endures! If they slay him, when the sun sets I shall be dead! I'll not live a moment after him!' Then they went to tell her father. Then her father summoned the lad into his presence, together with his daughter, and the lad came into his presence, and his dignity made an impression on the chief, and he embraced him and kissed him all over. And he said to him: 'Tell me about yourself; see!

You are like a son to me,' And he said to him: 'I am a son of an officer of the land of Egypt. And my mother died and my father took another wife; and she began to hate me, so I ran away from her.' Then he gave him his daughter to wife, and he gave him a house and fields, and also herds and everything nice.

Now sometime later the boy said to his wife: 'I am doomed to three fates, crocodile, snake, or dog.' Then she said to him: 'Have the dog following you killed,' but he said to her: 'Do not(?) ask that! I will not kill my dog! I have reared him from the time he was little.' And she took to keeping close watch over her husband, and not allowing him to go out alone.

Now indeed on the same day that the lad had left the land of Egypt to wander abroad, the crocodile, his fate had departed(?) ———— therein(?) ————, and he settled down opposite the town where the boy was, with his wife(?), dwelling (?) in the sea. Now a sprite lived there. The sprite would not let the crocodile go forth, nor would the crocodile let the sprite go out to wander; but when the sun arose they would begin to fight, both of them, each and every day, for the space of three full months.

Now after some days had passed the boy sat in his house, having a holiday. Then, after the night breeze had subsided(?), the boy lay down on his bed, and sleep overcame him. And his wife filled a jar with wine and another with beer. Out came a snake from its hole to bite the boy, while his wife sat sleepless at his side. Thereupon the jars toppled over(?) before(?) the snake, and he drank and became drunk; and he rolled over on his back, and his wife cut him up with her knife. Then she wakened her husband . . . and she said to him: 'See! Your God has delivered one of your fates into your hand! He will protect you from the other two(?)!' Then he made sacrifice to Re, praising him and extolling his might day by day.

Now after some days had passed the boy went out to stroll through his estate(?) for recreation. His wife did not go, but his dog followed him. Then his dog acquired speech, and said: 'I am your fate(?)' Then he ran from his dog towards the sea, and descended to the water, still fleeing from his dog. Thereupon the crocodile seized(?) him, and took him to the place where the sprite was. And the crocodile said to the boy 'I am your fate who has followed you! For three full months until now I have been fighting with the sprite. But see! I will let you go if ———— to fight ———— and you cheer(?) for me: "kill the sprite!" Now if you see the ————'

Now when the next day dawned, there came . . . (the rest is lost)." (3)

6

"And the Great God Laughed"

The Egyptian Wit

In one type of Egyptian story there is a pronounced Rabe-
laisian touch—its theme is a mythological episode about the
gods, but reworked in a free, bawdy style. This treatment
does not indicate any lessening of faith, much less contempt
for established cultus. The stories arise out of a stratum of
popular entertainment, rather than temple ceremony, and
are more akin to mediaeval miracle plays and popular saints'
lives than to sacred scripture. The gods are stereotyped, almost caricatured, as the villains, heroes, lovers, or buffoons
of a kind of set *opera bouffe*. Whether any live dramatic
tradition underlies the pieces rendered below is not known;
but without doubt we are dealing with the oral tradition of
the people.

THE TALE OF THE TWO BROTHERS

This story is only the opening episode of a longer account of the doings of two lesser deities, Anpu (Anubis), and Bata. The same basic motif was borrowed by other literary traditions, including the Hebrew (cf. Genesis 49) and the Greek (e.g. Bellerophon), and used as an "opening device" by means of which a story-teller could launch a composite yarn. Apart from the fact that the crisis is not satisfactorily resolved, the episode can be extracted with little difficulty from the rest of the narrative.

Now they say there were once two brothers, born of the same mother and father, the elder called Anpu and the younger Bata. Anpu had a house and a wife, and his younger brother Bata lived with him after the manner of a son. . . . Now his young brother was a very strong man, there was none like him in the entire land; in fact the strength of a god was in him. Now when many days had passed after this, his younger brother was tending his cattle, as was his daily custom, and he would break off and go home to his house every evening, loaded with all the herbs of the field . . . and he would lay them before his elder brother who was sitting with his wife eating and drinking. Then he (i.e. Bata) would go and sit in his stable, surrounded by the cattle . . . .

Now at seed-time his elder brother said to him: 'Let us harness the horses for ploughing, for the fields have come forth ready for planting. So come you to the fields with seed, because we shall begin planting in the morning.' So he said to him. Thereupon the younger brother did everything his elder brother had commanded him to do. And when dawn broke next day they went to the field with their seed, and started planting with merry hearts.

Many days later, when they were still in the field, they ran out of seed, and he said to his younger brother: 'Haste you and fetch us seed from the town.' So he made haste, and his younger brother found his elder brother's wife sitting doing up her hair. Then he

said to her: 'Get up and get me some seed, that I may hurry back
to the field, for my elder brother is waiting for me! Don't dawdle!'
Then she said to him: 'Go and open the grain bin and get what
you want; but do not make me leave off doing my hair.' Then the
young man entered his stable, took a large container, for his intent was to take much seed, loaded it with barley and came out.
Then she asked him: 'How much do you have on your shoulder?'
And he said to her: "Three *khar* of barley, two of wheat, altogether
five.' Then she said: 'Great strength is in you! I have been watching you every day!' Now her desire was to know him carnally.
She stood up and grabbed him, and said to him: 'Come! Let us
spend an hour lying together! It will be good for you! I shall make
you fine clothes!' Then the young man became as furious as a
southern panther because of the evil suggestion she had made to
him, and she was very frightened. Then he upbraided her saying:
'Look here! You are like a mother to me, and your husband is
like a father! He is older than I, and he brought me up! What is
this great sin you have suggested? Don't say it to me again! I shall
tell it to no one, I shan't even let it out of my mouth to anybody!'
And he took up his load and went off to the field. When he
reached his elder brother, they set to work once more.

Now afterward at the time of evening the elder brother broke
off work and went home to his house, while his younger brother
herded the cattle, and loaded himself with various good things of
the field. And he drove his cattle before him to put them into
their barn which was in the town. And his elder brother's wife
was terrified by the response she had gotten, so she took some fat
and suet and made herself look as though she had been grievously
beaten, in order to tell her husband: 'It was your younger brother
that beat me.' And her husband had broken off work at eventide
as was his daily habit; but when he arrived home he found his
wife fallen prostrate, feigning illness. She did not pour water on
his hands as was her custom, nor had she lit the lamp before
him: his house was in darkness, and she was lying vomiting. Her
husband said to her: 'Who has had words with you?' Then she
said to him: 'No one except your younger brother. When he came
to fetch you seed he found me sitting alone, and he said to me:
"Come! Let us spend an hour lying together! Let down your

hair!" So he said to me, (but) I did not listen to him. "Am I not your mother? Is not your elder brother like a father to you?" I said to him. Then he was afraid, and he beat me to prevent me from telling it to you. Now if you let him live I shall die. . . .' Then his elder brother became like a southern panther. He sharpened his knife, took it in his hand, and stood behind the door of his stable to kill his younger brother when he came at nightfall to put his cattle into the barn.

Now when the sun set, he (i.e. the younger brother) loaded himself with all the herbs of the field as was his daily habit, and went off. And when the lead cow entered the barn, she said to her master: 'Behold! Your elder brother is waiting for you with his knife in hand to kill you! Run away from him!' Then he harkened to what his lead cow said. And the second cow entered and said the same thing. And he looked under the door of his barn, and he saw the feet of his elder brother as he stood behind the door, with his knife in his hand. And he threw his load upon the ground, and began to flee on the run,[1] and his elder brother came after him with his knife. Then his younger brother prayed to Re-harakhte saying: 'O my good lord! Thou art the one that judges the guilty from the innocent!' Then Re heard his every prayer, and Re caused a great body of water filled with crocodiles to appear between him and his elder brother; and one was on one side, and the other on the other. And his elder brother beat his hands twice because he was not able to slay him. Then the younger brother called out to him from the bank, saying: 'Wait there until daybreak, and when the sun comes up I shall be judged with you in his presence, and he will decide who is in the right and who is in the wrong. Because I shall never live with you again, nor shall I live in any place where you are . . .'

When day broke and Re-harakhty rose, and they could see each other, the lad upbraided his elder brother saying: 'What do you mean by coming after to me to slay me unjustly, without listening to what I had to say? And I moreover your younger brother! And you are like a father to me, and your wife is like a mother to me! Is it not the case that, when you sent me to fetch seed, your

---

1. Literally, "he betook himself to run away in order to flee."

wife said to me: "Come! Let us spend an hour lying together"?
See! She has twisted the story for you!' Then he revealed to him
everything that had happened between him and his wife; and he
took an oath by Re-harakhty, saying: 'Your coming to slay me
unjustly with your knife was (simply) at the instigation of that
dirty slut!' And he took out a reed knife and cut off his phallus,
and threw it into the water, and the cat-fish swallowed it, and
he became soft and weak. And his elder brother was exceedingly
heart-broken, and stood weeping aloud, unable to cross over to
where his younger brother was because of the crocodiles. . . .

And his elder brother went home with his hand on his head,
and covered in dust (i.e. in mourning). And when he got home,
he slew his wife, and threw her to the dogs, and sat mourning for
his younger brother. . . . (1)

BOOK OF THE HEAVENLY COW
(OPENING PERICOPE)

Unlike many Near Eastern peoples, the Egyptians lacked
a "Flood Story." They did, however, preserve a curious tradition about how the sun-god had once long ago decimated
what he had created by means of his "Eye," i.e. his fiery disc,
personified in the form of a fierce lioness. In the present
work this gruesome tale is embellished by an account of how
Re lost and then regained control of his Eye, and this ribald
addition is used in turn to explain the origin of a particular
cultic act. Such "aetiologies," i.e. stories advanced as ex-
planations of names, customs, or natural phenomena the real
origin of which is unknown to the society in question, are
very common in ancient Egyptian literature.

Once they say when the Majesty of Re who came into being by
himself was king of men and gods at the same time, men plotted
evil against him. Now His Majesty L.P.H. was old, his bones were
silver, his limbs gold, his hair was genuine lapis lazuli. Then His
Majesty perceived the evil which was being plotted against him

by men, and he said to those who were in his train: 'Summon me my Eye, Shu and Tefnut, Geb and Nut, together with the Fathers and Mothers who were with me when I was in Nun, and also my god Nun, and let him bring his entourage with him. Bring them in secret(?); let not men see it, let not their hearts fail . . .' Then these gods were brought, and touched the earth in His Majesty's presence . . . Then said they to His Majesty: 'Speak to us and we will listen.' Then said Re to Nun: 'O thou eldest god from whom I took my being, and ye ancestor-gods! Behold! mankind who came into being from my Eye has plotted evil against me. Tell me what you would do about it. See, I am seeking your advice. I cannot kill them until I hear what you have to say about it . . . . Lo, they have already fled away to the hills, their hearts being afraid because I might speak to them.' Then said they to His Majesty: 'Let thine Eye go forth to smite those who have fallen into sin . . .'

So she went down in the form of Hathor. This goddess returned after she had slain men upon the highlands, and the Majesty of this god (Re) said: 'Welcome in peace, O Hathor, you who act for the creator(?)! Come to me(?)!' But this goddess said: 'As I live! I have actually overpowered mankind! This feels good to me!' . . .

Then Re said: 'Summon me swift and speedy messengers, that they may run like a body's shadow(?),' and they were brought in at once. Then said the Majesty of this god: 'Haste to Kebebu and bring me ochre(?) in large quantities'; and it was brought to him. Then the Majesty of this god made 'Big Curl' who is in Heliopolis grind up this ochre(?) while the priestesses were crushing grain for beer. When the ochre(?) was added to the beer mash it looked like human blood, and 7000 jarfuls were made . . . Now when the day dawned on which the goddess was going to continue to slay mankind . . . the Majesty of Re said: 'It is well! I shall protect mankind from her . . . carry it (the beer) to the place where she intended to slay men.' Then the Majesty of the king of Upper and Lower Egypt Re rose very early, in the dead of night, to pour out the 'Sleeping Potion,' and the fields were flooded to a depth of three palms with the liquid through the power of god. Then came this goddess in the morning, and found the stuff flooding the fields. Her face brightened at the sight and she drank. It felt good to her, and she went away drunk, not being able to distinguish mankind. Then said the Majesty of Re to this goddess: 'Welcome in peace, O charming one! (i3myt)' And that is how beautiful girls came to be in the town of Yamu. Said the Majesty of Re about this goddess: 'The Sleeping Potion shall be made for her at the seasonal festivals of the year(?), and it shall be reckoned to my priestesses(?).' That is how it came to be that all men make Sleeping Potion as a reckoning of the priestesses(?) at the Feast of Hathor since the dawn of creation . . . (2)

THE TRIAL OF HORUS AND SETH

This work is what might be called a set of variations and permutations on a well-known theme, rather than a "canonical" version of the myth itself. The myth of the life and death of Osiris, and his avenging by his son Horus, offered wide scope for embellishment. The Trial of Horus and Seth takes as its point of departure that part of the story which describes how the two principals have temporarily ceased warring and have submitted themselves to litigation. The prize is inheritance of the "office" of Osiris, i.e. the right to rule the land. The court comprises a number of well-known gods who tend on the whole to favour Horus's claim; but the presiding judge is Re-harakhty the sun-god, who is outspoken in his support for Seth. In a number of loosely-related episodes the litigants state and restate their arguments, or engage in trial by combat, while the court vacillates in its judgement in a most unexemplary fashion. Individual gods are clearly lampooned or caricatured: Isis is a talkative busybody, Seth a fool who resorts only to brute strength, Neit a sharp-tongued old woman, Horus a wily stripling, Re-harakhty a moody, sulky old man, and so on. The whole, though teeming with mythological allusions (too numerous to be elucidated here), is a bawdy treatment which consciously strives for humour.

The case of Horus vs. Seth, the secret of forms,[2] the greatest princes that ever were . . . (after some initial wrangling, the following suggestion is made to the court:) 'Do not let us take a decision in our ignorance. Have a letter sent to great Neit, the god's mother; whatever she says we will do.' . . . Then the Ennead said to Thoth in the presence of the Eternal Lord (i.e. the sun-god): 'So write a letter to great Neit, the god's mother, in the name of the Eternal Lord, the Bull-who-is-in-Heliopolis.' Then Thoth said: 'I will, yes, I will,' and he sat down to write the letter, and he said: '. . . this humble servant is spending sleepless nights on behalf of Osiris, governing the Two Lands day in day out, while Sobek is set for eternity! What are we to do for the two men who for eighty years now have been in court without anyone being able to decide their case? So write and say what we should do.'

Then great Neit, the god's mother, sent a letter to the Ennead as follows: 'Give the office of Osiris to his son Horus, and don't commit such great and unworthy crimes, or I shall get angry and the sky shall fall upon the earth; and someone should tell the Eternal Lord, the Bull-who-is-in-Heliopolis, to compensate Seth double; give him your two girls Anath and Astarte,[3] and put Horus on the seat of his father Osiris.' Thereupon great Neit, the god's mother's latter reached the Ennead . . . and it was delivered to Thoth. Thereupon Thoth read it out in the presence of the Eternal Lord and the entire Ennead, and they said with one voice: 'This goddess is right!'

Then the Eternal Lord got angry at Horus and he said to him: 'You have a miserable body! This office is too big for you, you boy with bad breath!' Thereupon Anhur got furiously angry, and so did the entire Ennead and the Council of Thirty L.P.H., and the monkey-god Baba jumped up and said to Re-harakhty: 'Your shrine is empty!' Thereupon Re-harakhty was hurt at the retort he received, and he lay down on his back very heart-sick. And the Ennead went outside and screamed in the face of the god Baba,

2. An epithet of several gods, probably referring to the holiness of their being or to the forms in which they manifest themselves.
3. Both Anath and Astarte are Canaanite goddesses who had been generally accepted in the Egyptian pantheon of the period.

and said to him: 'Get out! This sin you have committed is too much!' and they went off to their tent. Then the great god spent a day lying on his back in his pavilion, very heart-sick and alone. And after a long time Hathor, mistress-of-the-sycamore, came and stood before her father the Eternal Lord, and bared her vulva before his eyes. Thereupon the great god laughed at her.

And he got up, and sat with the Ennead, and said to Horus and Seth: 'Say your piece.' Then said Seth, the very strong, the son of Nut: 'Me, I'm Seth, the strongest one of the Ennead. I slay the enemy of Re daily at the prow of the "Barque of Millions"; no other god can do that! I should get the office of Osiris.' Then they said: 'Seth the son of Nut is right.' But Anhur and Thoth shouted: 'Should the office be given to the uncle when the legitimate son is present?' Said Banebdjed, the living god: 'But should the office be given to the boy when his elder brother Seth is present?' .... Thereupon Isis got angry at the Ennead, and took a divine oath in front of the Ennead: 'As Nut and divine Neit live! And as Ptah-tenen lives, he-of-lofty-feathers, the curber(?), the horned one of the gods(?)! These matters should be laid before Atum, the great prince who is in Heliopolis, and Khepry too who is in his barque!' And the Ennead said to her: 'Don't be annoyed. Right will be done to him who is in the right; everything you said shall be done.' Thereupon Seth the son of Nut became angry with the Ennead, and Seth said to them: 'I will take my scepter of 4,500 *nms* (in weight) and I will kill one of you each day. . . . I will not contest this case in court if Isis is present.'

Thereupon Re-harakhty said to them: 'Cross over to Center Island, and judge them there, and tell Anty the ferryman not to take any woman across who looks like Isis.' So the Ennead crossed over to Center Island, and sat down to have a meal. Then Isis came along and went up to Anty the ferryman as he was sitting beside his boat, (now she had changed herself into an old woman who walked with a limp(?), with a small gold seal in her hand); and she said to him: 'I have come to you in order that you may take me across to Center Island; because I am taking a pot of flour to the young lad. He has been tending a few herds on Center Island for five days now, and he's hungry.' He said to her: 'They told me not to take any woman across.' She said to him:

'It's because of Isis that they told you what you just said.' He said to her: 'What will you give me for taking you to Center Island?' Thereupon Isis said to him: 'I will give you this cake.' Then he said to her: 'What good is your cake to me? Am I to take you across to Center Island, when they have told me not to take any woman across, just for your cake?' Then she said to him: 'I will give you the gold seal in my hand.' He said to her: 'Give me the gold seal,' and she gave it to him. Then he took her across to Center Island, and she walked away under the trees.

. . . Then Seth looked up and saw her coming in the distance. And she uttered her magic spell and changed herself into a girl with a beautiful figure—there was no one like her anywhere in the land. Thereupon he loved her so much that it hurt exceedingly. And Seth got up from sitting lunching with the Great Ennead, and went to meet her; (now no one else had seen her except him). Then he stood behind a tree and called out to her: 'Here I am waiting for you, O beautiful one!' She said to him; 'So, my mighty lord? Me, I was the wife of a cowherd, and I bore him a male child; and when my husband died the boy began to tend his father's herds. But a foreigner came and sat in my barn, and said something like this to my boy: "I am going to give you a beating, and take away your father's herds, and throw you out!" So he said to him; but I would like you to take his side.' Thereupon Seth said to her: 'Shall the herds be given to the foreigner when the man's son is present?' [4] Then Isis changed herself into a kite, and flew up and perched on the top of a tree, and called out to Seth: 'Weep for yourself! It's your own mouth that said it! It's your own clever lips that have judged you! What's wrong with you now?' Thereupon he began to weep, and he went off to the place where Re-harakhty was (still) weeping. . . .

Then, when evening had come, Re-harakhty and Atum, the Lord of the Two Lands, the Heliopolitan, sent to the Ennead as follows: 'You are sitting there, but what are you doing, really? As for the two lads, you're making them spend a lifetime in court. When my letter reaches you, you are to put the White Crown on the head of Horus, the son of Isis, and you shall appoint him in

---

4. The irony of Seth's remark depends on a pun between the words "office" (i^3t) and "herds" (i^3wt).

the place of his father Osiris.' Thereupon Seth became terribly
and fiercely angry, and the Ennead said to Seth: 'Why are you
angry? Should one not act in accordance with what Atum says,
the Lord of the Two Lands, the Heliopolitan . . . ?' Then the
White Crown was fixed on the head of Horus son of Isis. Thereupon Seth screamed angrily in the face of the Ennead: 'Is the
office to be given to my little brother, while I, his elder brother,
am present?' And he swore an oath, saying: 'The White Crown
should be taken off the head of Horus son of Isis, and he should
be thrown into the water so that I can contend with him for the
office of Ruler!' Then Re-harakhty did so(?).

Thereupon Seth said to Horus: 'Let's change ourselves into
hippopotami, and go underwater in the middle of the Great Sea.
The one who comes up within three full months will not be given
the office.' Then both of them went under the water. Thereupon
Isis sat down and sobbed: 'Seth has killed my boy Horus!' And
she brought an armload of string and made a rope; she brought
a dbn of copper and cast it into a harpoon, and attached the rope
to it, and hurled it into the water at the place where Horus and
Seth had gone down. Then the metal pierced her son Horus, and
Horus screamed out: 'Help me, mother Isis, my mother! Tell your
weapon to release me: I am Horus, son of Isis!' Thereupon Isis
called out to the weapon: 'Release him! See, it is my boy Horus.'
And her weapon released him. Then she hurled it into the water
again, and it pierced the body of Seth, and Seth screamed out:
'What have I done to you, sister Isis? Tell your weapon to release
me: I am the brother of mother Isis!' And Isis took pity on him
exceedingly. . . . Thereupon Isis called out to her weapon: 'Release him! See, it's the uterine brother of Isis that you have
pierced!' And the weapon released him. . . .

Then the Ennead said: 'Summon Horus and Seth and let them
be judged.' And they were brought before the Ennead. Then, in
the presence of the Ennead, the Eternal Lord said to Horus and
Seth: 'Come, listen to what I tell you. Eat, drink, and let us have
a respite, and put an end to this daily wrangling once and for all!'
Then Seth said to Horus: 'Come, let's take a holiday at my house,'
and Horus said to him: 'I will, yes, I will.' Now when evening
had come a bed was spread for them, and both of them lay down.

Now in the night Seth made his penis erect, and put it between Horus's buttocks, and Horus put his hand between his buttocks, and received Seth's semen. Then Horus went to tell his mother Isis: 'Help me, Isis my mother! Come, see what Seth has done to me.' And he opened his hand and let her see Seth's semen. With a scream she took her weapon and cut off his hand, and threw it into the water, and conjured for him a hand to make up for it. Then she got some sweet salve and put it on Horus's penis, and made it erect and put it into a pot, and made his semen drop into it. Then she went carrying Horus's semen in the morning to the garden of Seth, and she said to Seth's gardener: 'What vegetables does Seth eat here with you?' And the gardener said to her: 'He does not usually eat any vegetable here with me except lettuce.' So Isis put Horus's semen on them (i.e. the lettuces). Then Seth came, as was his daily custom, and ate the lettuce which he usually ate; and he arose pregnant by the semen of Horus. And Seth went to tell Horus: 'Come, let's go, and I will contest the case with you in court.' Then Horus said to him: 'I will, yes, I will.' And both of them went to court, and stood before the Great Ennead, and they were told: 'Say your piece.' Then Seth said: 'Give me the office of Ruler, L.P.H., because as for Horus here, I have played the male role with him.' Then the Ennead screamed aloud, and belched and spat in Horus's face. But Horus laughed at them, and Horus took a divine oath: 'Everything that Seth said is wrong! Summon the semen of Seth, and let us see where it answers from; and summon mine too, and let us see where it answers from.' So Thoth, the master of divine speech, the true scribe of the Ennead, laid his hand on Horus's elbow and said: 'Come out, O semen of Seth!' and it answered him from the water which is in the middle of the cucumber bed. Then Thoth laid his hand on Seth's elbow and said: 'Come out, O semen of Horus!' and it said to him: 'Where shall I come?' and Thoth said to it: 'Come out through his ear.' Thereupon it said to him: 'Shall I, who am divine seed, emerge through his ear?' So Thoth said to it: 'Come out through his brow.' Then it emerged as a golden disc on Seth's head; and Seth was very angry, and he stretched forth his hand to seize the golden disc. But Thoth took it from him and set it as a diadem on his (own) head.

Then the Ennead said: 'Horus is in the right, Seth is in the
wrong.' Thereupon Seth got very angry, and he screamed aloud
when they said 'Horus is in the right, Seth is in the wrong.' And
he took a great, divine oath: 'The office shall not be given him
until he is put outside with me, and we shall cut ourselves some
stone boats, and both of us will race. The one who beats the other
shall be given the office of Ruler, L.P.H.' So Horus cut himself a
boat of cedar, and plastered it with gypsum, and put it into the
water at evening when there was no one about to watch. Then
Seth saw Horus's boat, and thought it was stone; and he went to
the mountain, and lopped off a hill-top, and cut himself a stone
boat 138 (cubits) in length. Then they got into their ships in the
presence of the Ennead, and Seth's boat sank beneath the water.
So Seth turned himself into a hippopotamus, and tried to sink
Horus's boat. But Horus seized his weapon and hurled it at the
body of Seth; and the Ennead said. 'Don't throw it at him!' Then
Horus retrieved his harpoon. . . .

Thoth spoke to the Eternal Lord: 'Have a letter sent to Osiris,
and let him judge the two lads.' Said Shu, son of Re: 'Right a
million fold, what Thoth said to the Ennead!' So the Eternal
Lord said to Thoth: 'Sit down and write a letter to Osiris, and
let's hear what he has to say.' Then Thoth sat down to take a
letter to Osiris, as follows: '. . . . Inform us what we are to do for
Horus and Seth, so that we do not act in our ignorance.' Then,
after some time, the letter reached the king, the son of Re (Osiris)
. . . and he screamed when the letter was read in his presence.
Then he sent his reply very quickly to the place where the Eternal
Lord and his Ennead were: 'Why is my son Horus being cheated,
when I am the one that gives you strength? It is I, is it not, that
creates barley to nourish the gods, as well as the cattle who follow
the gods? No other god or goddess found himself able to do it!'
Thereupon the letter of Osiris arrived at the place where Re-
harakhty was . . . and it was read aloud before him and the
Ennead; and Re-harakhty said: 'Alright, write me a reply to
Osiris's letter quickly, and say to him in the letter: "If you had
never existed, if you had never been born, barley would still have
come into being!"' Then the Eternal Lord's letter reached Osiris,
and he (sic) read it aloud in his presence; then he sent back to

Re-harakhty as follows: 'Very, very fine is all that you have done, you who founded the Ennead, yet who let Truth slip into the Underworld! Now you—yes, you!—look at the way things stand. The land where I am is filled with fierce-eyed messengers who fear neither god nor goddess. I send them out and they bring back the hearts of all those who have committed sin, and they remain here with me. Why do I stay here and rest in the West, while all of you to a man are out there? Which of you is stronger than I? Yet you (sic) actively devised evil. Now when great Ptah, South-of-his-Wall, Lord of the Life of the Two Lands, created the heaven, did he not say to the stars which were in it: "Each night you must set in the West, in the place where king Osiris is; and after the gods" he said to me, "the patricians and the plebeians shall also go to rest where you are?" ' Now when some time had passed Osiris's letter arrived at the place where the Eternal Lord was, along with the Ennead, and Thoth received the letter and read it aloud before Re-harakhty and the Ennead. Then they said: 'Everything he said is quite right . . .' Then Seth said: 'Have us taken to Center Island so that I can contest the case with him.' So he went to Center Island and the verdict was given in favour of Horus.

Then Atum, the Lord of the Two Lands, the Heliopolitan, sent word to Isis: 'Put a neck-fetter on Seth and bring him.' So Isis put a neck-fetter on Seth and brought him under guard. Then Atum said to him: 'Why did you prevent the two of you from being judged, all the while trying to take the office of Horus for yourself?' And Seth said to him: 'Utter fantasy, my good lord. Have Horus son of Isis summoned, and give him the office of his father Osiris.' So they brought Horus son of Isis, and put the Double Crown on his head, and set him on the seat of his father Osiris, and said to him: 'Thou art the good king of Egypt, thou art the good lord, L.P.H., of every land for ever and ever eternally!' Thereupon Isis shouted out to her son Horus: 'Tho art the good king! My heart rejoiceth when thou brightenest the land with thy rays!' Then said great Ptah, South-of-his-Wall, Lord of the Life of the Two Lands: 'What shall be done for Seth, now that Horus has been put on the seat of his father Osiris?' Then Re-harakhty said: 'Let me have Seth, the son of Nut, and he will live with me and be my boy; and when he thunders in the sky people will fear him . . .' (3)

7

"Read the Stele Which I
... Have Written for Posterity"

The Idea of History

Philosophical speculations on the proper interpretation of
the term "history" have filled countless volumes. It is not
my wish here to repeat any definition, or to make a futile
attempt to phrase a new one. Rather I shall try to merely
outline the ancient Mesopotamian's attitude toward the past.
In doing this I am, of course, using ideas and categories alien
to ancient Mesopotamia, for, as mentioned in the Introduction, the whole mode of thinking in the ancient Orient was
entirely different from our own in modern Western civilization. To illustrate: in the realm of the conceptualization of
the past, a word for history is absent in Sumerian and Akkadian. This lack does not mean that the ancient Mesopotamians were not interested in their past. That the contrary
is true is abundantly clear from the various kinds of Meso-

potamian texts written about past events and the frequent reference to past events in contemporary documents. Rather the absence of the word "history" symbolizes an entirely different approach to the past, or to what we call history. Here in this half we will probe deeper into the Mesopotamian mind, and perhaps at least gain a general idea of their concept of history.

A note: in this chapter we shall normally restrict ourselves to the Assyro-Babylonian idea of history, for this is better documented. Much of what will be said will, however, also apply to Sumer for the cultures were really part of one complex.

A basic principle in understanding Assyro-Babylonian ideas about history is the attitude they held toward the relation between earthly events and heavenly powers. To the Assyro-Babylonian the interaction of heavenly and earthly affairs was so basic a consideration that they hardly ever felt it necessary to mention it specifically. In the mind of the ancient Mesopotamian there was virtually no distinction between heaven and earth. Every mundane matter depended on divine action, from the appointment of a king to the birth of an infant. All was controlled by celestial powers.

This recognition immediately explains one aspect of the Assyro-Babylonian idea of history—the lack of reference to "causes" of the kind a Western historian looks for. To an Assyrian or Babylonian the reasons for any event were self-evident: the gods had made it so. Rarely do the historians feel it necessary to state this explicitly. Thus in Babylonian chronicles one finds such statements as the following:

The first year of Mushezib-Marduk: On the seventeenth day of the month Ab Kudur-Nahhunte, king of Elam, was captured during a revolution and killed. For ten months Kudur-Nahhunte had ruled Elam. Humban-nimena ascended the throne in Elam. In an unknown year Humban-nimena, king of Elam, mustered the troops of Elam and Babylonia and fought against Assyria at the city Halule. He forced the Assyrians to retreat. (1)

Why was there a revolution? How could Elam recover so quickly from such turmoil and inflict a defeat upon Assyria at Halule? These questions, which we immediately ask, were of no concern to the Babylonian scribe. If we could ask him these questions, he would most certainly reply that the gods willed it, and perhaps add a diatribe on our stupidity for not knowing this. This basic assumption of divine causation is occasionally expressed, however, and then there is no doubt how the ancient Mesopotamian viewed "causes." Thus the Assyrian king Sennacherib, in describing his part in this same battle at Halule, says:

The king of Elam brought together a great allied force . . . They closed ranks with the king of Babylon and marched forth to do battle against me. With the strength of the god Ashur, my lord, I fought with them in the plain of the city Halule. I defeated them. (2)

Ignoring for the moment the claim of both to have won the same battle, it is abundantly clear in the Assyrian inscription that the victory came about as a result of the god Ashur working through his chosen servant, the Assyrian king. Thus the Assyrians and Babylonians were not concerned with recording *why* things happened. Everyone knew why.

Related to divine causation is the belief in divination. Not only did the ancient Mesopotamians believe that all events on earth were controlled from heaven, but also that signs or omens were given by the gods before events occurred. Thus the death of the king might be preceded by an eclipse of the sun. If a human being wished to know in advance what the gods intended, he had to learn how to read these signs. The art of predicting the future through divination became a highly developed science among the ancient Mesopotamians. A wide range of phenomena were considered appropriate for this purpose but the most popular were movement of the stars, astrology, and the appearance of a sacrificed sheep's entrails, extispicy. Here is just a sampling from the large scholarly treatises on this subject:

If the planet Jupiter is visible during an eclipse of the moon, it means all is well for the king. (3)
If the cords of the middle finger of the lung are four in number, the king will make love to many women. (4)

Often the meaning of the omen is interpreted in terms of historical events:

If the intestines look like the head of the monster Huwawa, it is the omen of Sargon who became lord of the land. (5)
If the tissue inside the umbilical fissure of the liver is thick, it is the omen of Shulgi who captured Tappa-Darah. (6)

In each of these cases the omen is favourable; the gods have answered "Yes" to the petitioner's question. In particular note that the two historical omens mean nothing more than this, and are not to be taken in the sense that the same events will repeat themselves over again. The petitioner will not, like Sargon, become lord of the land or, like Shulgi, capture a foe called Tappa-Darah. They simply mean that the petitioner should undertake to do whatever he was asking about. Here there is no question of a cyclical view of history, in the Assyro-Babylonian mind—there was no set pattern by which the same events would occur over and over again. The practice of divination simply meant that the gods, when they approved of something or decided on some course of action themselves (notice the absence of determinism here—the deities act of their own free will), would reveal their opinion or intention through such media as animal entrails or the movement of stars.
The belief that each event, though unique, could be pre-

dicted by qualified humans is particularly evident from a group of texts called "prophecies." [In fact, these are pseudoprophecies for they are composed after the event (*vaticinium ex eventu*).] The "prophet," wishing to establish his credibility, "predicts" events that have already happened. Additional features of these texts are the anonymity of the rulers, the fact that a reign is either "good" or "bad," and the use of technical phrases employed in the omen literature. Here are excerpts from one such text:

A prince will arise and rule for eighteen years.
The land will be at peace and fare well, the people will enjoy prosperity.
The gods will ordain good things for the land, the winds will be favourable.
Field and furrow will yield abundant crops,
Animals and grain will be plenteous in the land.
There will be rains and floods (to irrigate the fields), the people of the land will enjoy themselves.
But that prince will die by the sword in a revolution.

A prince will arise and rule for thirteen years.
There will be an Elamite attack on Babylonia
And the booty of Babylonia will be carried off.
The shrines of the great gods will be destroyed, Babylonia will suffer a defeat.
There will be confusion, disturbance, and disorder in the land;
The great will be abased and another man, who is unknown, will arise;
He will seize the throne as king and massacre his nobles with the sword;
With the corpses of half the extensive army of Babylonia,
He will fill the lowlands, plains, and level ground of Tupliyash;
The people will suffer need and hardship.

A prince will arise but his days will be short and he will not be lord of the land.

After a break the text resumes in the middle of a "good" reign:

That king will be lord of the Four Quarters of the world . . .

His people will enjoy prosperity . . .

He will re-establish the regular offerings to the Igigi gods, which had ceased . . .

The winds will be favourable . . .

The cattle will lie down in green pastures,

The winter-grass will last until summer and the summer-grass will last until winter

A prince will arise and rule for three years.

Cities will be overthrown, dwellings will be destroyed.

There will be rebellions and . . .

There will be hostilities committed against Babylonia.

The rites of the temple Ekur in the city Nippur will be abandoned.

The Amorites will put that prince to the sword.

A prince will arise and rule for eight years.

The shrines of the gods will fall into disrepair,

The rites of the great gods will not be re-established.

There will be no rains or floods, . . .

The people will suffer misfortune, . . .

The rich will be impoverished, the poor will become rich,

The rich man will beg from the poor man, . . .

. . . mother will speak falsely to daughter . . .

The fortunes of the land and people will take a turn for the worse.

Pestilence will ravage the land, the king will bring hardship upon the land. (7)

The author of this composition has provided enough details, such as the number of years a reign lasted, to enable one well-versed in Mesopotamian history to calculate which period he

is referring to. The Book of Daniel contains passages like this (8:23 25 and 11.3–45) in which the appearance of anonymous kings serves as an introduction to vague descriptions of their reigns. Here too only a person well-read in the period's history can identify the historical personages and events to which Daniel refers. It is not surprising that the same genre should appear in both civilizations for the Hebrews, like the Babylonians, had no cyclical concept of history but regarded every event as unique.

If the documents seen so far have helped us understand the general assumptions underlying the Assyro-Babylonian view of the past, it still remains to ask why they were interested in the past, and why and how did they write historical literature, and what forms their writings took? Their motives were both practical and idealistic; each gave rise to various genres. Practical historical records contained omens which were interpreted in terms of past events. These were compiled to assist one in understanding the future. Records of ominous features which appeared just before major events were carefully compiled for future reference. If the same ominous features should appear again, the initiated could then examine their records to discover what event in the past they had portended. Though this may seem to us highly fanciful, to the ancient Babylonian historical omens served a real and practical purpose.

Another pragmatic type includes documents written for didactic or propagandistic motives. The Assyrian royal inscriptions were written with the intention of overwhelming both subjects and foreigners with the unsurpassed might and valour of the monarch. Authors of these documents did not hesitate to exaggerate facts or even lie to achieve this end. Thus, in a passage from Sennacherib's inscriptions translated at the beginning of this chapter, he claims victory in a battle against the Elamo-Babylonian coalition at Halule while the more factual and reliable Babylonian Chronicle records that the Assyrian lost. In this case, as in so many, the Assyrian annals are not at all to be believed—they are, and are intended to be, propaganda. The Assyrians certainly did not win at Halule.

Among Babylonian historical-literary texts there is a genre
—the pseudo-autobiographies—which is intended to teach.
These are literary accounts of historical events told in the first
person, by the king. Unlike the royal inscriptions, they are
composed after the death of the king in a highly literary style.
The best known of these is the Cuthean Legend of Naram-Sin.
After a lengthy description of the misfortunes that befell
Naram-Sin (c. 2254–2218 B.C.) and the reason for them, the
author concludes with an exhortation to a later prince to heed
the document which has been written and from it learn how
to conduct himself:

. . . read the stele
Which I, Naram-Sin, son of Sargon
Have written for posterity!
After Sargon, my father, passed away,
After Rimush and Manishtusu passed away,
I, Naram-Sin, became controller of the land.
When days had passed,
When years had gone by,
The goddess Ishtar had a change of heart
And the hordes of Umman-manda rode down from the mountains.
In this crisis I consulted the great gods,
Ishtar, Baba, Zababa, Anunitu,
Hanish, Shullat, Shamash, the warrior;
I summoned the diviners and issued orders,
I slew seven and again seven lambs
And set up the holy reed altars.
The diviners declared to me:

The slaying of the lambs and the setting up of the altars was
in preparation for extispicy, examination of animal entrails to
learn the will of the gods. Unfortunately, the beginning of
their answer, through the diviners, is missing. But when the

text resumes the diviners are still speaking and it is apparent
that they find the omens confusing:

"Do not try to evaluate the omens yourself, restrain yourself
Until the great gods have made their answer clear.
Remember Enmerkar, the ancient king, upon whom the god
    Shamash pronounced a severe judgement!
His judgement and decision with regard to Enmerkar—his ghost, the
    ghosts of his children,
The ghosts of his family, the ghosts of his offspring, the ghosts of
    the offspring of his offspring, it was decreed by Shamash, the
    warrior,
Lord of Upper World and Lower World, lord of the Anunnaki gods,
    lord of ghosts,
That all of them should drink muddy water, that they should not
    drink clear water;
That his wisdom and weapons had detained, defeated, and destroyed
    a certain army
On a stele he should not leave in writing."

This is the end of the diviner's speech. The point is that an
ancient king Enmerkar had not waited for a clear answer from
the gods and as a result had not achieved a victory which he
could record on his stele. Naram-Sin accepts the admonition
for the text continues:

I did not stir myself nor did I ride forth.

Then comes a lengthy description of the Umman-manda
hordes who have invaded Naram-Sin's kingdom:

People with the bodies of partridges, men with the faces of ravens,
Thus had the great gods created them.
In a region whose city the gods had built
Tiamat, the sea-dragon, had suckled them,
Their mother, the mistress of the gods, had taken good care of them,
In the mountains they grew up, matured, and reached full stature.
There were seven kings, brothers, famous for handsomeness,
Their multitude numbered three hundred and sixty thousand.

The description continues with the names of the seven kings
and the details of their invasion, which spreads from Anatolia
to Iran. In the face of this terrible horde Naram-Sin, despite
the divine injunction, finds it hard to restrain himself any
longer:

I summoned a knight and gave him orders,
I handed him a thorn and pin saying:
"Prick with the thorn, pierce with the pin,
If blood comes forth, they are men like us,
If blood does not come forth, they are genii, demons,
Shades, evil spirits, creatures of the god Enlil."
The knight brought back this report:
"I pricked with the thorn,
I pierced with the pin and blood came forth!"
I summoned the diviners and issued orders,
I slew seven and again seven lambs
And set up the holy reed altars,
I consulted the great gods
Ishtar, Baba, Zababa, Anunitu,
Hanish, Shullat, Shamash, the warrior.
But the will of the great gods still would not permit me to march!
So I said to myself, this is what went through my mind:
"What lion ever practised divination?
What wolf ever consulted diviners?
I will go of my own accord, just like a brigand!"

Thus does Naram-Sin defy the gods with terrible results:

At the beginning of the first year,
I sent forth one hundred and twenty thousand troops and not one
    of them returned alive.
At the beginning of the second year I sent forth ninety thousand
    with the same result.
At the beginning of the third year I sent forth sixty thousand, seven
    hundred, with the same result.
I was confused, bewildered, dismayed, worried, upset,
So I said to myself, this is what went through my mind:
"What have I left to the (glory of my) reign?
I am a king who has not kept his land secure,
A shepherd who has not kept his people secure.
How could I have been so precipitous as to have gone forth!
Now panic, night, death, plague, shivers,
Terror, chills, financial losses, hunger,
Famine, insomnia—innumerable ills—have come down upon my
    people.
Above, in the city, a flood has appeared,
Below, in the fields, a flood has come."

The god Ea, lord of the deep, opened his mouth to speak,
He said to the gods, his brothers:
"O great gods, what have you done?
You gave the command and I brought the flood.
But now have mercy, do not remain angry."

At the New Year's festival, at the beginning of the fourth year,
With the wisdom of the god Ea, with the advice of the great gods,
I presented holy sacrifices for the New Year
And examined the holy omens.
I summoned the diviners and issued orders,
I slew seven and again seven lambs
And set up the holy reed altars,
I consulted the great gods

Ishtar, Baba, Zababa, Anunitu,
Hanish, Shullat, Shamash, the warrior.
The diviners declared to me:

In the following broken passage the diviners at last give a
favourable reply and Naram-Sin meets the enemy in battle and
is successful. At the end of the text appears a long exhortation
by Naram-Sin to future rulers to heed the lesson that one must
not disobey the will of the gods as revealed through omens.
Even if an enemy should invade and ravage one's land, one
must stay inside the city walls until the omens say it is time
to attack. Naram-Sin, like Enmerkar, at first disobeyed this
cardinal principle and suffered severely. He exhorts future
princes to learn from his and Enmerkar's example.

There were as well idealistic motives at work in the history-
writing we find. Indeed there is a whole series of Babylonian
chronicles, from which we have already quoted, which was written by scribes who wished to record as accurately as possible the
major events of their times. They do not hesitate to note
Babylonian victories or defeats and therefore, when they state
that the Elamo-Babylonian coalition won at Halule and not
the Assyrian (see the beginning of this chapter) we are more
inclined to believe them. We owe a great debt to these con-
scientious and industrious scribes—our whole reconstruction
of Neo-Babylonian and Neo-Assyrian history rests upon their
works. From a literary point of view, however, these chronicles
—dry, prosaic accounts of events—leave much to be desired.

The Babylonians also wrote historical works of literary
merit, which should be included with these idealistically motivated documents. Some epics of a partially historical nature
also belong in this category. Although there are mythological
and legendary aspects to such a work as the Gilgamesh Epic,
for example, there must be a core of historical truth to such
episodes as the Expedition to the Cedar Forest; the modern
reader must be impressed with the determination of Gilgamesh
to perform this deed in the face of tremendous obstacles.

In essence the ancient Mesopotamian regarded the study of

his past as a practical, useful pursuit which could assist him in everyday life and could be used for didactic and propagandistic purposes. On the other hand at least some ancient Babylonian scribes recognized the inherent value of studying the past and keeping careful, accurate records of events. Still others found inspiration in past personages and events for poetic expression. Thus, to the Assyrian and Babylonian, history was on the one hand a useful pursuit and on the other an end in itself.

8

"Enlil Subdued All Lands Under Him"

The Idea of Imperialism

The idea of imperialism, one of the oldest ideas in recorded history, appeared in western Asia over four thousand years ago, and was given practical expression there before 1000 B.C. The concept evolved naturally in Mesopotamia from the early rivalry over border lines and irrigation ditches between autonomous city-states. From these disputes in the third millennium B.C. emerged the conquest by one state of one or more neighbouring city-states. This in turn developed into the conquest of not simply small communities but large tracts of land. The "conquest" at this early stage, though, seems to have had little more motivation than the acquisition of foreign wealth by plunder and the punishment of troublesome neighbours, and it remained for the Assyrians in the first millennium B.C. to develop the idea of permanent control over conquered regions by means of provincial administration. With this development, Imperialism was transformed from an idea into a reality.

Lugalzagesi (c. 2360 2335 B.C.) is the first Sumerian military leader to show signs of thinking beyond the capture of a few neighbouring city-states. For, apart from being able to claim control over several such districts (e.g. Uruk, Nippur, Umma, Ur, Larsa, and Lagash), this king boasts:

When the god Enlil, king of the lands, gave to Lugalzagesi sovereignty over Sumer, caused Sumer to look directly to him (for leadership), subdued all lands under him, made the entire region from east to west submit to him; at that time Enlil created for him a clear passage from the Lower Sea (Persian Gulf), along the Tigris and Euphrates, to the Upper Sea (Mediterranean). In the entire region from east to west Enlil made him free of opposition. He made the people of the lands lie down in peaceful pastures like cattle and supplied Sumer with water bringing joyful abundance. (1)

The submission of not only Sumer but the entire region from the Persion Gulf to the Mediterranean (including modern Iraq and Syria) is no mean achievement and one would expect more details about such a feat. Indeed, one is sceptical in the absence of such information and the enigmatic form of this passage. Did Lugalzagesi actually control the whole territory? Some have suggested that "Enlil created for him a clear passage" refers to formation of a caravan route and nothing more. Be that as it may, certainly the ideal behind this passage is actual political predominance in an area stretching far beyond the traditional boundaries of Sumer, and thus we see the seed of imperialism. Note as well that even this embryonic imperialist carefully claims to have brought peace and prosperity to the conquered territories.

The seed of imperialism sown in the time of Lugalzagesi germinated with the advent of Sargon (2334–2279 B.C.) and the foundation of a completely new dynasty in Sumer centred at Akkad. That Sargon was a kind of Napoleon is evident from the tales and legends told about him and the numerous and valorous deeds attributed to him. Even if some individual accomplishments are denied him by modern historical research, the fact remains that an outstanding personage must have given rise to such an impressive tradition. By far the most intriguing event of his fifty-four year reign is his campaign to the Mediterranean Sea and the Taurus Mountains in Anatolia, referred to briefly in two of his inscriptions:

The god Enlil gave to Sargon the Upper and Lower Sea (Mediterranean Sea and Persian Gulf). (2)

Sargon, the king, bowed down to the god Dagan in Tuttul and prayed. Dagan gave to him the Upper Land (Syria): Mari, Yarmuti, Ebla, as far as the cedar forest and the mountains of shining metal. (3)

The cities Tuttul, Mari, Yarmuti, and Ebla were in Syria. Dagan was a god connected with that region. The cedar forest refers to the famous cedars of Lebanon and "the mountains of shining metal" is a name for the Taurus range, a source of silver. Is Sargon saying he conquered Syria as far as the Taurus range? If so, it is not expressed clearly, nor is this as detailed a description as one would expect for such a momentous accomplishment. Thus we are in the same position as we were with Lugalzagesi—the inscriptions are suggestive but ambiguous. But for Sargon we have further sources for this problem. In the tradition that built up around Sargon after his death we find a pertinent statement in a chronicle:

In his eleventh year Sargon conquered the entire western land. He brought it under one authority. He erected his statues in the west. He brought across the western booty by raft. (4)

This, a much clearer statement than hitherto encountered, provides at the same time a clear reason for Sargon's expedition

—to bring back booty. This also illuminates the reference to cedars and silver in the earlier inscriptions. In the Babylonian plain, an area poor in natural resources, strong beams and precious metals were non-existent. The only way to obtain them was by trade with or conquest over foreign lands. This same motivation for the campaign is found in another legend about Sargon, the so-called "King of Battle Epic," which describes the difficulties of a merchant colony in Anatolia which turns to Sargon of Akkad to free them from the oppression of a neighbouring ruler. Sargon, in answer to their plea, sets out on the long and difficult road to Anatolia. When he arrives, there is a confrontation with the trouble-maker and apparently a peaceful settlement. References to exotic goods to be found in Anatolia indicate that these were an important factor for the campaigners.

However much one might quibble about the veracity of details in the tradition of Sargon's imperialist expansion, it is the first time the idea of imperialism has been clearly expressed. It remained for the Assyrians to adopt this early Mesopotamian idea, give it practical expression, and to try to develop it to its logical conclusion, conquest of the world. Already one of the early Assyrian rulers, Shamshi-Adad I (1813–1781 B.C.), emulated Sargon of Akkad by staking a claim to the west:

I received the tribute . . . of the king of the Upper Land (Syria) within my city Ashur. I established my great name and my steles in the land Lebanon on the shore of the Great Sea (Mediterranean). (5)

From other, unimpeachable sources we know that there were several autonomous kingdoms in Syria at this time and that Shamshi-Adad's boast, at best, probably refers to a friendly exchange of gifts. Military conquest is virtually out of the question. But what he could only claim with words, his successors to the Assyrian throne would take with the sword, for some centuries later Assyria produced a series of formidable monarchs who would become notorious for their imperialistic ambition and blood-curdling cruelty. One of these was Shalmaneser I (1274–1245 B.C.) in whose inscriptions is found a detailed description of an attack on Hanigalbat, a district in Syria:

When, at the command of the great gods and in the supreme strength of the god Ashur, my lord, I marched to the land Hanigalbat, I opened up the most difficult of paths and the worst passes. Shattuara, king of the land Hanigalbat, with the assistance of the troops of the Hittites and Ahlameans, captured the passes and watering-places before me. When my troops became thirsty and exhausted, their troops made a vicious attack in full force. But I struck back and defeated them. I killed countless numbers of their numerous troops. As for Shattuara, I pursued him westward at arrow-point. I slaughtered their hordes. 14,400 of them which survived I blinded and carried off. I conquered nine of his fortified cult-centres together with his capital city and I completely destroyed one hundred and eighty of his cities. I butchered like sheep the troops of the Hittites and Ahlameans, his allies. (6)

Thus did Assyria attempt to fulfill the imperialistic ideals inspired by Lugalzagesi and Sargon of Akkad. The motivation for the mass mutilation and wanton destruction characteristic of the Assyrian conquerors was not sheer vindictiveness, however. Their frightfulness was calculated both to discourage other lands from resisting them and to weaken their unfortunate victims by mutilating or carrying off warriors and by ravaging towns and farmland so that potential enemies could find no sustenance or defence. This latter practice is particularly apparent from another passage in Shalmaneser I's inscriptions in which the conquest of Uruatri (later known as "Urartu"), a district in eastern Turkey, is described:

In three days I made all of the land of Uruatri bow down at the feet of the god Ashur, my lord. I selected some of their young men to enter my service. I imposed for eternity heavy tribute upon the mountainous regions.

The city Arinu—the well-founded holy city, the city at the base of the mountains, the city which had previously rebelled and disregarded the god Ashur—with the support of Ashur and the great gods, my lords, I conquered that city. I destroyed it and sowed salt over it. I gathered some of its dirt and piled it up in front of the gate of my city, Ashur, for posterity. (7)

One must recognize the wisdom of bringing captive young men to Assyria, there to be trained in Assyrian customs and ideals and eventually, if possible, returned to their native land as friendly allies. Apart from this, however, one can only condemn both on ethical and tactical grounds, the horrible mutilation and devastation. The most short-sighted part of early Assyrian foreign policy was the dreadful destruction of long-term sources of revenue. Once a city had been destroyed, its population and movable wealth carted off to Assyria, and its farmland sown with salt, there would be no tribute to pay to anybody for a long time. The cunning collector of taxes knows that in levying imposts there is a point of diminishing returns. Once he goes beyond that the victim can no longer operate profitably and therefore cannot pay his taxes. It took the Assyrians most of their history to learn this very basic rule. Hundreds of years after Shalmaneser I we find kings of Assyria still following essentially the same practice of ruling an empire by *razzia*. They boast of control over huge tracks of land stretching as far west as the Mediterranean, as far north as the Caucasus, and as far east as Iran, but this control continues to consist of little more than plundering expeditions emanating from the Assyrian capital. This dichotomy is vividly portrayed in a passage from the inscriptions of Ashurnasirpal II (883–859 B.C.) in which a campaign east and north of Assyria is described:

With the support of the god Ashur, my lord, I left the city Tushhan and taking with me the strong chariots, the cavalry, and the crack troops, I crossed the Tigris on rafts. Marching all night I eventually approached the city Pitura, the fortified city of the people of the land Dirra. The city was very difficult of access since it was surrounded by two walls and its fortification stuck up like a mountain-peak. With the supreme might of the god Ashur, my lord, and with the power of my army and fierce warfare I fought with them. For two days, beginning before sunrise, I thundered against them like the god Adad, god of storm, and rained down upon them flames. With might and main my soldiers flew at them like the bird-god Zu, the storm-bird. At last I captured the city. I felled eight hundred of their soldiers with the sword and cut off their heads. Many soldiers I captured alive but the remainder I burnt. I carried off valuable booty from them. I formed a pile of live bodies and heads at the entrance to the city gate. I hung up on stakes seven soldiers at the entrance to the city gate. I completely destroyed the city, turning it into a hill of ruins. I burned their young men and women.

I conquered the city Kukunu which is at the entrance to the pass of Mount Matni. I felled seven hundred of their soldiers with the sword and carried off much booty from them. I conquered fifty cities of the land Dirra; massacred their people; carried off their booty; captured fifty soldiers alive; and burnt and completely destroyed the cities. Thus did I overwhelm them with my lordly splendour.

I left the city Bitura and descended to the city Arbaki in the interior of the land Habhi. They took fright in the face of my royal splendour and they abandoned their cities and walls. They ascended Mount Matni, a mighty mountain, to save their lives. I marched after them. I cut down one thousand of their warriors in difficult mountain terrain. With their blood I dyed the mountains red and with their corpses I filled the gorges and crevices of the mountain. I captured two hundred soldiers alive and cut off their hands. Two thousand of them I carried off as captives and their herds and flocks without number I brought away.

The cities Iyaya and Salaniba, fortified cities belonging to the city Arbaki, I conquered. I massacred their people and carried off their booty. Two hundred and fifty strongly walled cities of the lands Nairi I completely destroyed, turning them into hills of ruins. I

reaped the harvest of their land and deposited the barley and straw
in the city Tushha . . .

I am Ashurnasirpal, great king, strong king, king of the universe,
king of Assyria, . . . valorous warrior who marches about with the
support of the god Ashur, his lord, and who has no rival among all
princes of the Four Quarters (i.e. the world), the king who has subdued at his feet the entire region from the East Tigris area to the
mountains of Lebanon and the Great Sea (Mediterranean). (8)

The titles which appear at the end of this passage are much
grander than the actual achievements described. The conquest
of Syria as far as Lebanon and the Mediterranean is described
(in an earlier passage) in terms similar to this short excerpt
from the trans-Tigridian endeavours and, as must be obvious
to the reader, the "conquest" is basically a gigantic *razzia*.
Ashurnasirpal milks the land for everything it is worth and
commits horrible atrocities in order to frighten neighbouring
cities into submission.

But the Assyrians have learned something since the time of
Shalmaneser I. They have agreements with some of the native
rulers of these "conquered" districts by which they are required
to send regular tribute to the Assyrian monarch. In return the
Assyrians keep their blood-thirsty armies out of their districts.
It is an ancient and massive form of the "protection racket."
The Assyrians were wise enough to provide security for these
native rulers and supported them in time of need. Thus, in the
following passage Ashurnasirpal describes how he avenged one
such trusted ally, Amme-bala:

The nobles of Amme-bala, son of Zamanu, rebelled and killed
him. To avenge Amme-bala I marched and the rebels took fright in
the face of my shining weapons and supreme lordship. I received
from them chariots equipped with the harness and trappings for
soldiers and horses, four hundred and sixty draft horses, two talents
of silver, two talents of gold, one hundred talents of tin, one hun-

dred talents of bronze, three hundred talents of iron, one hundred bronze pots, three thousand bronze saucers, bowls, cauldrons, one thousand linen garments with multicoloured trim, tables, chests, couches decorated with ivory and gold—the treasure of his palace— two thousand oxen, five thousand sheep, his sister with her rich dowry and the daughters of his nobles with their rich dowries. (9)

But even in seeking vengeance on behalf of a faithful ally the Assyrian, unable to restrain his cupidity, empties the dead ally's treasury in the process of avenging him! Note, by the way, the low status of women in Assyria as evidenced by their being placed last in this list of booty.

More than a century must pass before the Assyrians, becoming more far-sighted in their foreign policy, begin to realize their imperialistic dream. Only the last few Assyrian kings really attempted to create a provincial administration with locally-appointed governors (on occasion native rulers were allowed to hold such an office, particularly in remote areas) and Assyrian garrisons of soldiers. It is interesting to compare a passage from this later period (from an inscription of Sargon II, 721–705 B.C.) which, like the last one translated, describes how the Assyrian monarch treated one of these native rulers. In this case it is a Mannean ruler whom Sargon wins to his side not by terrorism but by promises of aid. Here is Sargon's own account:

I left the land Parsuash and approached the land Missi, a province of the land of the Manneans. Ullusunu, together with the people of his land, awaited my campaign in his fortress Sirdakka to wholeheartedly do me service. Like officials and governors of Assyria he supplied an abundance of flour and wine for the sustenance of my army. He sent to me his eldest son with peace offerings and entrusted to me his stele for the confirmation of his sovereignty. From him I received as tribute great draft horses, herds and flocks and he begged me to avenge him. He, together with the nobility and officials of his land, beseeched me to bar the Kakmeans, hostile enemies, from his land; to defeat Ursa, king of Urartu, in the bat-tlefield; to restore the scattered Manneans to their place; and to let them stand in victory over their enemies; that is to achieve all their desires. While presenting this petition they crawled in my presence on all fours like dogs. I took pity upon them, heard their petitions, heeded their entreaties, and said to them, "Put your minds at rest!" I promised them to overthrow the land Urartu, to restore their boundaries to their former positions, and to bring relief to the harassed Manneans by means of the surpassing strength which had been given to me by the gods Ashur and Marduk, who had made my weapons prevail over all the princes of the universe. They took heart.

In the presence of Ullusunu, their king and lord, I laid a rich table and made his throne higher than that of Iranzu, his own father. I sat them with the people of Assyria at the joyful table and before Ashur and the gods of their land they blessed my sov-ereignty. (10)

The change in Assyrian tactics is evident here both in the factual account of what each ruler did for the other (the Mannean supplied the Assyrian army with food like any Assyr-ian governor and in return the Assyrian promised to defeat his enemies) and in the mutual courtesy accorded to one another (the Assyrian provides a banquet and the Manneans recognize his sovereignty). But the Mannean is still the weaker partner, which he openly admits, crawling in the Assyrian's presence on hands and knees like a dog.

Lest one think these last Assyrian kings have completely changed however, here is a passage from the annals of Sargon's successor, Sennacherib, in which the traditional barbarity of these imperialists appears in all its horrible detail:

On my eighth campaign I ordered a march to Babylon. When the Babylonians heard of the approach of my expedition they were overcome with dreadful fear. They opened the treasury of the tem-ple Esagil and brought out the gold, silver, and gems of the gods

Marduk and Sarpanitu in great abundance. They sent them to Ummanmenanu, king of Elam, and communicated to him this message: "Come to Babylon to our aid! Stand by us! Be our support!" Now the king of Elam was a rash fellow who had neither insight nor wisdom (and he accepted the bribe and came to their aid) . . . I prayed to Ishtar of Nineveh and Ishtar of Arbail, my sustaining goddesses, for the conquest of my strong enemies and they quickly heeded my prayers and came to my aid. Angrily roaring like a lion I dressed in my armour and put on my head the helmet, the proper attire for battle. In my exalted battle-chariot which lays low my enemies I rode quickly in my anger . . . I thundered like a storm, I roared like Adad, the god of storm. By command of the god Ashur, the great lord, my lord, like the onset of a powerful tempest I rushed against the enemy. With the weapon of the god Ashur, my lord, and the onslaught of my raging warfare I turned them around and forced them to retreat . . . The nobles of the king of Elam who wear a golden dagger at the waist and whose arms are bedecked with sling-bracelets of reddish gold—like fat steers to which nose-ropes are attached—these I quickly slaughtered . . . I slit their necks like sheep and cut their precious throats like thread. Like a mighty flood of the storm season . . . I made their blood run down over the broad earth. My swift thoroughbreds, the team of my chariot, plunged into the mass of their blood as though into a river and the wheels of my battle-chariot, which overthrows rogues and criminals, were bathed in blood and entrails . . . I cut off their beards thereby destroying their dignity. I cut off their hands like bunches of ripe cucumbers. I took the sling-bracelets of gold and another shining metal, which were on their arms. With sharp swords I cut their belts and took away the gold and silver daggers at their waists.

Like a bull the terror of my battle overthrew Ummanmenanu, king of Elam, and Shuzubu, king of Babylon. Like the pursued young of a dove their hearts were fluttering. They passed their urine and voided their excrement in their chariots. To save their lives they pushed on, crushing the corpses of their own soldiers . . . (But I overtook them). At my feet they petitioned my lordship: "Leave us our lives that we may forever sing your praises!" When I saw that they had voided their excrement in their chariots I left them alone so that their lives were spared. (11)

Terrorism supplemented by appeasement and provincial administration in the later period were two of the major tactics employed by these first empire builders. Another, which they had discovered already in the Middle Assyrian period, was the transportation of troublesome subjects, which practice, as time passed, increased in popularity with the Assyrian monarchs. Large sections of the population of a conquered but recalcitrant area would be carried off to other parts of the empire, particularly back to Mesopotamia, where they were frequently pressed into labour in newly created settlements. The classic example of this policy appears with the Chaldean monarchs of the Neo-Babylonian empire, heir to the Assyrian empire after the fall of Nineveh in 612 B.C. The greatest king of this dynasty, Nebuchadnezzar II (604–562 B.C.), has won everlasting notoriety in the Bible because of his transportation of large numbers of Judeans to Babylonia after the conquest of Jerusalem in 587 B.C. (II Kings 25:1–30 and II Chronicles 36:17–21). Unfortunately we do not have the Babylonian version of this event, but we do have the original account of the first capture of Jerusalem by this king a few years earlier (597 B.C. —II Kings 24 and II Chronicles 36:9f.). In the translation of this document, which is a chronicle, I have included the events of the years leading up to it.

The fourth year of Nebuchadnezzar II (601/600 B.C.): The king of Babylonia called up his army and marched to the west. He marched about victoriously in the west. In the month Kislev (November/December of 601 B.C.) he took his army's lead and marched to Egypt. When the king of Egypt heard the news he called up his army. They fought one another in the battlefield and both sides suffered severe losses. The king of Babylonia and his army turned and went back to Babylon.

The fifth year (600/599 B.C.): The king of Babylonia stayed home and refitted his numerous horses and chariotry.

The sixth year (599/598 B.C.): In the month Kislev (November/ December of 599 B.C.) the king of Babylonia called up his army and marched to the west. He dispatched his army from the west and they went off into the desert. They plundered extensively the possessions, animals, and gods of the numerous Arabs. In the month Adar (February/March of 598 B.C.) the king went back home.

The seventh year (598/597 B.C.): In the month Kislev (December/ January) the king of Babylonia called up his army, marched to the west, and laid siege to the city of Judah (i.e. Jerusalem). On the second day of the month Adar (March 16, 597 B.C.) he took the city. He captured its king (Jehoiachin) and a king of his own choice (Zedekiah) he appointed in the city. He brought vast tribute into Babylon. (12)

Thus by destruction and mutilation, transportation of peoples, provincial governors, and garrisons, and pacts with indigenous leaders the Assyrians (and later the Babylonians) fully developed the idea of imperialism originated by the ancient Mesopotamians in the third millennium B.C. Before the collapse of their political power they had conquered all of the civilized world stretching from the highlands of Iran to the shores of Europe and Africa. An idea, which had been proven practical, thus became so firmly embedded in the minds of men that no subsequent ruler in this area was content until he had attempted to at least repeat the Assyrian achievement.

9

"Rebellions in Assyria and Babylonia"

Revolution as Resistance to Imperialism

No people submit willingly to imperialism. A history of imperialism can be at the same time a history of resistance to it. Down through history the conquerors have labelled such struggles "revolutions"; the conquered have called them "wars of independence." Thus the great conflict of the eighteenth century in the history of the United States is referred to as the "American Revolution" in British textbooks but as the "War of Independence" in American texts.

The history of Babylonia under Assyrian rule provides an excellent example of such a struggle. The Assyrians regarded all resistance to their imperialistic ambitions, be it by Babylonians, Syrians, Egyptians, or Hebrews, as revolution. For these people, however, the motivation was neither criminal nor seditious but simply a desire for independence. For Babylonia the fight was long and arduous, stretching over a century and involving the sack of her capital and the desecration of her most sacred religious shrine. The Babylonians have not left, as have other revolutionary struggles, a record of any lofty ideals or fiery oratory which might have evolved during this era, but the tale of stubborn determination which we do have, indicates that these factors must have been present.

The story begins in the reign of the Babylonian king, Nabu-nasir (747–734 B.C.). At his accession an independent Babylonia is so secure that the king can concern himself with some basic reforms. But in his third year (745 B.C.) Assyria, flexing its muscles after a dormant period, leads its armies into Babylonia as recorded in a Babylonian chronicle:

The third year of Nabunasir, king of Babylon: Tiglath-pileser III ascended the throne in Assyria. In that same year the king of Assyria went down to Babylonia, plundered the cities Rabbilu and Hamranu, and abducted the gods of the city Shapazza. (1)

For the remainder of the reign of Nabunasir, the Babylonian monarch is little more than an Assyrian puppet. But resistance was brewing, and boiled over at his death with the seizure of the throne, after some confusion, by Nabu-mukin-zeri (more generally known as Mukin-zer). He is the first in a series of "freedom fighters" in Babylonian history, whose main purpose was to drive the Assyrian army from Babylonian soil. Since these revolutionaries were also leaders of tribes of Chaldeans, a nomadic group which had settled in Babylonia sometime earlier, a second motivation was to gain control of the state for Chaldeans. The Assyrians tried to exploit this second motivation to their own advantage by attempting to persuade the Babylonians to turn against the Chaldeans. This is evident in the following report to Tiglath-pileser:

To the king, my lord, your servants Shamash-bunaya and Nabu-etir send greeting. May the gods Nabu and Marduk bless the king my lord!

On the twenty-eighth day we went to Babylon and stood in front of the Marduk Gate. We argued with the man of Babylon. . . . , servant of Mukin-zer the Chaldean, was beside him. They came out and while they stood with the Babylonians in front of the gate, we spoke to the Babylonians like this:

The gist of the argument, the details of which are not entirely clear, is that the Babylonians, who enjoy a privileged position in the empire, surely do not wish to be associated with Chaldeans. The report continues:

We argued at length with them . . . but eventually they would not even come out to argue in person with us. They just kept sending us messages. We said to them:
"Open the gate and let us enter Babylon!" They would not agree but replied: "You alone we would have admitted to Babylon." We asked: "When the king comes, what can we tell him? That the gate will be opened?" But they did not believe that the king would come. (2)

The letter continues to describe the arguments and counterarguments, but no conclusive agreement with the Babylonians is reached. It is a curious scene, the Assyrian officials standing at the walls of Babylon trying to reason the Babylonians into surrender. Exactly the same measure was used by a later Assyrian, Sennacherib, who sent his *rabshukeh* official to Jerusalem to persuade the Judeans to surrender (II Kings 18:17–19:8). The kernel of the Assyrian argument in our letter is that Mukin-zer is a Chaldean and the citizens of the city of Babylon surely do not wish to associate with him. This appeal to domestic differences was a clever tactic but it failed. The Babylonians continued to resist and Mukin-zer's movement had to be crushed by force as another report narrates:

We have penetrated the gates and are defeating them. Mukin-zer is defeated. Shuma-ukin, his son, is defeated. The city is taken. May the king rejoice! (3)

Thus ended the first attempt to regain Babylonian independence. Assyrian kings for a brief period after this reigned supreme in Babylonia, even claiming the hereditary title "king of Babylon," but then the second great Babylonian revolutionary, Merodach-baladan II, appeared. Indeed he appeared several times over the following years, popping up like a jack-in-the-box, stretching his appearances over the reigns of no less than four Assyrian kings! He actually gained independence for Babylonia for twelve years. But the Assyrian king, Sargon II (722–704 B.C.), finally ended this early phase in the revolutionary's career, as laconically reported in a Babylonian chronicle:

The twelfth year of Merodach-baladan: Sargon went down to Babylonia and fought against Merodach-baladan. Merodach-baladan retreated and fled to Elam. For twelve years Merodach-baladan had ruled Babylon. Sargon now ascended the throne in Babylon. (4)

But with Elamite aid, Merodach-baladan makes a comeback during the reign of Sennacherib (704–681 B.C.). Indeed (on this occasion), he has persuaded large sections of the Assyrian empire to join in this revolt. Thus in the Bible (II Kings 20:12–19 and Isaiah 39:1–8) we read of envoys sent by Merodach-baladan to Hezekiah, king of Judah, who successfully woo the Judean ruler to the cause, much to the anger of the prophet Isaiah, who realized that they would fail. The widespread insurrection, which stretched from the Persian Gulf through Syria to Judah, was crushed only after extensive and exhaustive campaigning by the Assyrians. At least two campaigns were required to deal with Merodach-baladan alone, for he had taken refuge in the swamps of southern Iraq. Here are excerpts from the two accounts in Sennacherib's inscriptions:

On my first campaign I brought about the defeat of Merodach-baladan, king of Babylonia, together with the army of Elam, his ally, in the plain of Kish. In the midst of that battle Merodach-baladan abandoned his position, ran away alone, and saved his own life. I captured the chariots, horses, wagons, and mules, which he had left behind on the battlefield. I gladly entered his palace in Babylon, opened up his treasury, and brought out as booty gold, silver, gold and silver vessels, precious gems, all of his innumerable and valuable property, his harem, palace officers, courtiers, male and female singers, all the artisans that served his palace. (5)

On my fourth campaign . . . I set out for the land Bit-Yakin. Merodach-baladan, whom I had defeated on a former campaign and whose forces I had scattered, took fright at the thundering noise of my mighty weapons and at my fiercely belligerent attack. Taking the statues of the gods of his entire land from their shrines and loading them on boats, like a bird he flew to Nagiteraqqi, an island in the sea (Persian Gulf). His brothers, offspring of his father's family, which he had abandoned at the seashore together with the rest of his countrymen I brought as prisoners out from the land Bit-Yakin, which is in the midst of swamp and reeds. I turned and completely destroyed his cities, making them into hills of ruins. (6)

Merodach-baladan appears in a bad light here, but these are enemy records. Whether the Babylonian hero was really such a coward, interested primarily in saving his own skin, must remain moot. Though his flight to an island in the Persian Gulf is the last we hear of him, the Assyrian, Sennacherib, continued to have difficulty with Babylonia and her ally the Elamites. Finally tragedy struck. Sennacherib's son and heir, who had been appointed king of Babylonia by his father, was captured in an Elamite raid. This marked the turning point in the Babylonian war of independence. Sennacherib was enraged by this act and in unbridled passion he marched to

Babylonia, captured the capital, and gave his soldiers licence to loot and destroy. Here is his account:

I swiftly marched to Babylon, which I was intent upon conquering. I blew like the onrush of a hurricane and enveloped the city like a fog. I completely surrounded it and captured it by breaching and scaling the walls . . . I did not spare his mighty warriors, young or old, but filled the city square with their corpses. Shuzubu, king of Babylon, together with his family and officers, I captured alive and took them to my country. I turned over to my men to keep the property of that city, silver, gold, gems—all movable goods. My men took hold of the statues of the gods in the city and smashed them. They took possession of the property of the gods. The statues of Adad and Shala, gods of the city Ekallati which Marduk-nadin-ahhe, king of Babylonia, had taken to Babylon at the time of Tiglath-pileser I, king of Assyria, I brought out of Babylon after four hundred and eighteen years. I returned them to the city Ekallati. The city and houses I completely destroyed from foundation to roof and set fire to them. I tore down both inner and outer city walls, temples, temple-towers made of brick and clay—as many as there were—and threw everything into the Arahtu canal. I dug a ditch inside the city and thereby levelled off the earth on its site with water. I destroyed even the outline of its foundations. I flattened it more than any flood could have done. In order that the site of that city and its temples would never be remembered, I devastated it with water so that it became a mere meadow. (7)

One is accustomed to read of this kind of Assyrian treatment of conquered cities outside of Babylonia. But Babylonian cities, and certainly Babylon itself, were not normally treated harshly. Despite the ancient and bitter rivalry between Assyria and Babylonia there were certain unspoken rules in the dispute. Their fight was one between brothers, not one between strangers. The Assyrians and Babylonians were related, ethnically, and the destruction of Babylon by Sennacherib was far beyond the bounds of the normal conduct of Assyro-Babylonian warfare. The Assyrians were soon to regret this extremely vindictive action.

After the devastation of Babylon there is a concerted effort to appease Babylonia by Esarhaddon, Sennacherib's son and successor, which indicates a feeling of guilt on the Assyrian side. The official penitence of the Assyrians is abundantly clear in Esarhaddon's inscriptions. In the following passage, unprecedented for its humble tone, appears a description of the destruction of Babylon by Sennacherib (similar to the one quoted above and therefore excluded from this translation), a statement that afterwards the Babylonian god Marduk was appeased and consented to allow the Assyrian to make amends, and then the favourable omens which appeared just before the reconstruction of the Babylonian temples was undertaken by the Assyrians:

Although Marduk had written (on the Tablet of Destinies) seventy years as Babylon's period of desolation, the merciful god was quickly appeased and changing the numeral around he commanded its resettlement to take place in eleven years. You, O Marduk, have faithfully chosen me, Esarhaddon, over my elder brothers to do the restoration. You have spread over me your good umbrella, you have overwhelmed all my enemies like a flood, you have slain every one of my opponents, and allowed me to achieve my heart's desire. You have commissioned me for the shepherding of Assyria in order that I might appease your great divinity and assuage your anger.

In my accession year . . . when I ascended in majesty the royal throne, there were good omens for me in heaven and earth. Marduk kept sending portents indicating that Babylon should be resettled and its shrines restored. Marduk commanded work to begin on the completion of the cult-centres, the restoration of the shrines, and the restitution of the rites of the temple Esagil, palace of the gods. Monthly Sin, the moon-god, and Shamash, the sun-god, when they appeared kept replying together "Yes!" to the divination priests' queries with regard to making amends to Babylonia.

With my wide understanding and extensive wisdom which the wisest of the gods, the prince Nudimmud, had granted me I carefully considered the resettlement of that city, the restoration of the shrines, and the decoration of the cult-centres . . . I mustered all the craftsmen and the entire land of Babylonia. With the axe they felled trees and reeds of the marshes or tore them out by the roots. I blocked off the flow of water from the Euphrates and directed it back to its normal river-bed . . . All the people of Babylonia I caused to work with trowels and on their shoulders I put hods . . . To demonstrate to the people Marduk's great divinity and to cause them to revere his lordship, on my own head I put a work-basket and carried it myself. (8)

This unheard of attempt at appeasement (note the exalted role of Marduk rather than Ashur) by the Assyrians failed. The Babylonians were more determined than ever to drive out the Assyrians. The beginning of the final and successful fight may be traced to the struggle between two Assyrian royal brothers, Ashurbanipal (668–627 B.C.) and Shamash-shuma-ukin (668–648 B.C.). To try and resolve the "Babylonian Question" for all time, Esarhaddon had appointed both his sons as kings, Ashurbanipal in Assyria and Shamash-shuma-ukin in Babylonia. No doubt the Babylonians were not appeased by this move, but when Shamash-shuma-ukin declared war on his brother, they supported him since it suited their own ends. Despite great endurance by the Babylonians during the extensive ravages of battle in their land, the Civil War was a failure for Shamash-shuma-ukin. In a Babylonian chronicle appears this passage (note the interruption of the celebration of the New Year Festival, chief Babylonian religious festival, as a sign of the serious disruptions):

The sixteenth year of Shamash-shuma-ukin: From the month Iyyar until the month Tebet the major-domo conscripted troops in Babylonia. On the nineteenth day of the month Tebet there were hostilities between Assyria and Babylonia. The king withdrew in the face of the enemy into Babylon. On the twenty-seventh day of the month Adar the troops of Assyria and Babylonia fought in

Hirlt. The troops of Babylonia retreated from the battle-field and a major defeat was inflicted upon them. However, there were still hostilities and warfare continued.

The seventeenth year: There were rebellions in Assyria and Babylonia. The god Nabu could not come from Borsippa for the New Year's procession of the god Marduk nor could the procession of Marduk take place.

The eighteenth year: The god Nabu could not come from Borsippa for the New Year's procession of the god Marduk nor could the procession of Marduk take place.

The nineteenth year: The god Nabu could not come nor could the procession of Marduk take place.

The twentieth year: The god Nabu could not come nor could the procession of Marduk take place.

. . . In the accession year of Nabopolassar there were rebellions in Assyria and Babylonia. There were hostilities and warfare continued. The god Nabu could not come nor could the procession of Marduk take place. (9)

From this chronicle one has an overall picture of the duration of the conflict, but the hardship involved for countless individuals is better illustrated by some documents from the Babylonian city Nippur. After Shamash-shuma-ukin had died, Nippur was invested by the Assyrian army and its unfortunate citizens reduced to actually selling their children for food. Records of these inhuman transactions have survived. Here are two typical bills of sale:

In the third year of Sin-sharra-ishkun, king of Assyria, Nippur was besieged and exit through the gate was impossible. With one shekel of silver one could buy a mere seah of barley (ten times the normal price) . . . People sold their children for silver. Gugalla said to Ninurta-uballit, son of Bel-usatu, "Take my young daughter Rindu and keep her alive. She shall be your maid. Give me six shekels of silver so that I can eat." Ninurta-uballit agreed and . . . took Rindu for six shekels of silver. (10)

Arad-Gula and Iddin-Nergal purchased Kalba-Baba . . . for twelve shekels of silver . . . from Nippur-reshat and Belit, his mother. Nippur-reshat and Belit guarantee that there has been and will be no other claim against Kalba-Baba. When the gate of Nippur was blocked, a time when with one shekel of silver one could buy a mere seah of barley, they voluntarily accepted the twelve shekels as the full purchase price for their son.

Dated at Nippur, this tenth day of the month . . . , in the third year of Sin-sharra-ishkun, king of Assyria. (11)

Whether or not any vengeance was later sought of the ghouls who profited from these transactions is not recorded. This phenomenon, by the way, reminds one of an even more horrible incident in the Bible—women eating each other's children during a siege (II Kings 6:24–31 and cf. Deuteronomy 28:52–57).

Success came at last to these stubborn people, and in 626 B.C., one hundred and five years after their struggle had begun, they put on the throne of Babylon, one Nabopolassar, the first Babylonian king for over a century who kept the crown until he died a natural death. This was the beginning of the greatest period in Babylonian history.

In the early years after Nabopolassar's accession the Assyrian army was still active in Babylonia, and the southern monarch had to battle them on home-ground. But gradually he pushed them back up the Tigris, until the conflict was taking place on Assyrian soil, and transformed the struggle from a war of independence to one of foreign conquest. The Babylonians had no qualms about having become the aggressors and continued to press the Assyrians until their very capital, Nineveh, was invested with the aid of the Medes and Umman-mandu. In due course Nineveh fell. For these momentous years we have a Babylonian chronicle:

The tenth year of Nabopolassar: . . . In the month Ab the troops of Assyria prepared for battle in the city Gablini and

Nabopolassar went up against them. On the twelfth day of the month Ab he fought against the troops of Assyria and the troops of Assyria retreated. He inflicted a major defeat upon Assyria and took much plunder. He captured the Manneans, who had come to their assistance, and the Assyrian officers. On that same day he captured Gablini . . .

In the month Tishri the troops of Egypt and the troops of Assyria went after the king of Babylonia as far as Gablini but they did not overtake him so they withdrew.

In the month Adar the troops of Assyria and the troops of Babylonia fought against one another at the city Madanu, a suburb of the city Arraphu, and the troops of Assyria retreated before the troops of Babylonia. The troops of Babylonia inflicted a major defeat upon them and drove them back to the Zab River. They captured their chariots and horses and in general took much plunder . . .

The eleventh year: The king of Babylonia mustered his troops, marched along the bank of the Tigris, and in the month Iyyar he encamped against the city Ashur. On the —th day of the month Sivan he attacked the city but did not capture it. The king of Assyria mustered his troops, pushed the king of Babylonia back from Ashur, and marched after him as far as Takritain, a city on the bank of the Tigris . . . The king of Babylonia stationed his troops in the fortress of Takritain. The king of Assyria and his troops encamped against the troops of the king of Babylonia which were stationed in Takritain and fought with them for ten days. But the king of Assyria did not capture the city. Instead the troops of the king of Babylonia, which had been stationed in the fortress, inflicted a major defeat upon Assyria. The king of Assyria and his army turned and went home . . .

The twelfth year: In the month Ab the Medes, after they had marched against the city Nineveh . . . captured Tarbisu, a city in the district of Nineveh . . . They went along the Tigris and encamped against Ashur. They attacked the city and . . . destroyed it. They inflicted a terrible defeat upon a large people, plundered and sacked them. The king of Babylonia and his troops, who had gone to help the Medes, did not reach the battle in time . . . The king of Babylonia and Cyaxares, king of the Medes, met one another by the city and they concluded a treaty . . . Cyaxares and his troops went home. The king of Babylonia and his troops went home . . .

The fourteenth year: The king of Babylonia mustered his troops and marched to the land . . . The king of the Umman-manda marched towards the king of Babylonia . . . They met one another. The king of Babylonia . . . Cyaxares . . . marched along the bank of the Tigris . . . They encamped against the city Nineveh. From the month Sivan until the month Ab—for three months— . . . they subjected the city to a heavy siege. On the . . .th day of the month Ab (July/August, 612 B.C.) . . . they inflicted a major defeat upon a large people. At that time Sin-sharra-ishkun, king of Assyria, perished . . . They carried off the vast booty of the city and the temple and turned the city into a hill of ruins. (12)

Thus did the Babylonians, with the aid of their allies, conquer Assyria. It is ironic that the oppressed had now become the oppressors. Indeed the Babylonians continued to campaign until they had conquered all of the region, including Egypt, that had once been the Empire of Assyria. The course of Babylonian history had now come full swing—once a victim of an imperial power, it, itself, was now an empire. The revolutionaries evolved into emperors.

10

"O Sin . . . Deliver Me!"

Nabonidus and the Fall of Babylon

In 539 B.C. Cyrus the Great of Persia marched into Babylon and ended independent government in ancient Iraq. Not until the twentieth century A.D. did this area regain its freedom. The events which brought about this catastrophe revolve around the last of the Babylonian monarchs, Nabonidus, one of the most unusual and puzzling figures in the ancient history of south-west Asia. No one, either ancient or modern, seems to have understood him and the motives that prompted his actions. It is not my intention here to discuss and analyze in detail either the character and career of Nabonidus or the extent of his responsibility for the fall of Babylon. Rather I wish to present a translation of the most famous version of this event, that of the priests of Marduk at Babylon, and briefly point out its basic fallacy. To do this it will be necessary to first provide the reader with some background, particularly in regard to Nabonidus' origin and his long sojourn at the Arabian oasis of Tema.

In some respects Nabonidus was a typical Neo-Babylonian monarch of the Chaldean line. Thus some of his royal inscriptions contain lengthy descriptions of temple reconstruction and little reference to non-religious matters. Here is a typical example:

Nabonidus, king of Babylon, patron of the temples Esagil and Ezida, worshipper of the great gods, I: Elugalgalgasisa, the temple-tower of the temple Egishnugal in the city Ur, which the ancient king Ur-Nammu had built but not completed so that his son Shulgi had to complete the work; I examined the inscriptions of Ur-Nammu and his son Shulgi and realized that Ur-Nammu had built but not completed that temple-tower so that his son Shulgi had to complete the work; now that temple-tower had become old. Using as a base the old foundation which Ur-Nammu and his son Shulgi had built, I repaired the damage to that temple-tower, as in olden days, with bitumen and baked brick. For the god Sin, lord of the gods of heaven and underworld, king of the gods, god of the gods who dwell in the highest heaven, lord of Egishnugal in the city Ur, my lord, I rebuilt it.

O Sin, lord of gods, king of the gods of heaven and underworld, god of the gods who dwell in the highest heaven, when you joyfully enter that temple may there be on your lips blessings for Esagil, Ezida, and Egishnugal, the temples of your great divinity. Reverence for your great divinity instill in my people that they might not sin against your great divinity. May their foundations be as firm as those of heaven. Deliver me, Nabonidus, king of Babylon, from sinning against your great divinity and grant me long life. In Belshazzar, my own offspring, my eldest son, instill reverence for your great divinity that he might have no sin and enjoy an abundant life. (1)

In one respect, however, this is not at all similar to royal inscriptions of other Neo-Babylonian monarchs, for the extremely exalted position accorded to the god Sin (the moon god) rather than Marduk is atypical. The reason for the special sponsorship of Sin by Nabonidus may be found in the king's origins: he was the son of Adad-guppi, a mysterious woman who had been a devotee of the god Sin at the Syrian city of Harran. We actually have an inscription of Adad-guppi (see Chapter 11) according to which she was ninety-five years of age when she died. Adad-guppi had actually lived the entire length of the Neo-Babylonian empire down to the ninth regnal year of her son, the last king of this line! But how is it that Nabonidus, with such provincial parentage, became king in Babylon? Our sources give no clear account, but it appears that after distinguishing himself in the service of the Babylonian court, Nabonidus took advantage of internal strife to seize the throne. Thus a late "prophecy" regards him as a usurper from Harran:

A rebel prince will arise,
The dynasty of Harran he will establish,
And he will rule for seventeen years.
He will oppress the land and cancel the (New Year's) festival of
    Esagil.

Evil will come forth to Babylonia (2)

There is no doubt about the bias of this pseudo-prophet. According to him Nabonidus had no right to the throne and his rule was a catastrophe. Such a view of this monarch is common in the sources available to us and may be attributed to his provinical background and his preference for the god Sin over the Babylonian god Marduk, a fact which enraged the priests at Babylon.

Even more mysterious than Nabonidus' seizure of the throne is his voluntary exile, for ten years of his reign was spent in an Arabian desert oasis, Tema. This curious fact is recorded in a Babylonian chronicle together with the result it had for the all important New Year's festival:

The seventh year of Nabonidus: The king was in the city Tema while the prince, Belshazzar, his officers and his army remained in Babylonia. The king did not come to Babylon in the month Nisan, the god Nabu did not come to Babylon, Marduk did not come out, and the New Year's festival was cancelled. The offerings were presented to the gods of Babylon and Borsippa as in normal times in Esagil and Ezida. The priest made a libation and inspected the temple. (3)

Essentially the same entry, with other details, appears for Nabonidus' entire period in Tema. Why did the monarch go to Tema, leaving his son Belshazzar behind to administer the state? There has been much speculation on this point and no unity of opinion. Our ancient sources themselves were divided in their views. Including them with the modern ideas, we find that the motivation for this bizarre behaviour is variously attributed to mental illness, physical illness, political, economic, and religious considerations. Some say he went there because he was mad—so the book of Daniel (4:28–37) where Nabonidus has been confused with the more notorious Nebuchadnezzar. Some say he went to recuperate from an illness in the salubrious desert air—so the "Prayer of Nabonidus" discovered among the Dead Sea Scrolls. And while some modern interpreters see various possible political or economic motives, others suspect a connection between Nabonidus' religious views and this voluntary exile among Arab nomads among whom the worship of the moon-god was popular.

Certainly the priests of Marduk believed religion to be the central issue in all that Nabonidus did. In brief, their view was that Nabonidus, in so ambitiously promoting the cult of the moon-god Sin, earned the disfavour of the supreme Babylonian god Marduk. His long sojourn in Tema, which caused the New Year's festival to be cancelled for ten years, was a particular source of the god's anger. All this brought about the king's downfall, for Marduk looked for another king to take control of Babylon and restore the religious rites appropriate to his cult. Such a ruler he eventually found in Cyrus the Great of Persia. Thus in 539 B.C., thanks to Marduk's patronage, the Persians under Cyrus marched into Babylon. Here is a poetic presentation of this version:

(Nabonidus made a statue of a god) which no one had ever seen in this country,
(He raised it up) and put it on a pedestal,
. . . he named it Nanna (the Sumerian name for Sin, the moon god).
(Its . . . was decorated) with lapis lazuli, a crown adorned its head,
. . . it looked like an eclipsed moon

(Nabonidus declared): "I will build him a temple, his abode will I fashion,
I will make its brick and lay its foundation,

Ehulhul is the name I will give it for all time.

"When I have completed that which I wish to build,
I will take his hand and put him on the pedestal.
Until I have finished this work, until I have achieved my desire,
I will abandon the festivals, the New Year's ritual I will discontinue."

He made its brick and designed the building's layout,
He made broad its foundation and made high its roof,
He made its surface shine with white gypsum and black bitumen.
An image of a fierce wild bull he put at the front as at Esagil.

After he had achieved his desire, a counterfeit construction,
After he had built this abomination, an unholy work—at the beginning of the third year
He entrusted affairs to his eldest son, Belshazzar,
The troops everywhere he put under his command.

He gave up everything and entrusting the sovereignty to his son
While he set out on a long journey;
The fighting forces of Babylonia advancing with him,
He headed towards the city Tema in the west.

He set out on a long trip. When he eventually arrived
He defeated the prince of the city Tema,
He butchered the herds of the inhabitants of town and country.
Then he entered and took up residence, he brought in the fighting
    forces of Babylonia.

The city he made outstanding, he built (a palace for himself),
Like the palace of Babylon he made it.

    After a long, but badly preserved passage in which the narra-
    tion of Nabonidus' return from Tema presumably appeared,
    the text continues:

While Cyrus is king of the universe, ruler of (all),
The kings of all lands bear his yoke,
Nabonidus has written on his steles: "At my feet (I have sub-
    dued . . .),
His lands have I conquered, his goods have I taken to my palace."

Nabonidus stands in the assembly boasting of his achievements:
"I am wise, I am learned, I have understood mysteries,
Although I am illiterate I have learned secrets.
The god Ilteri granted me a vision, he revealed to me everything,
I am privy to wisdom surpassing even that of
(The scholarly treatise) 'The Lunar Crescent of the Gods Anu and
    Enlil' which (the ancient sage) Adapa compiled."

Nabonidus would mix up the rituals, confuse the omens,
With regard to the most important rites he would say: "Enough of
    that!"
The designs of Esagil, the forms which the wise god Ea had fash-
    ioned,
He would look at these forms and utter blasphemies.
Nabonidus looked at the Lunar Crescent of Esagil and made a
    surprised gesture with his hands.
He gathered the scholars and said to them:
"Is this not the symbol of the one for whom the temple was built?

If it belonged to the god Marduk, the symbol would have been the
   Spade,
But the god Sin has designated it with the Lunar Crescent as his
   house!"

Zeriya, the bishop, crouching in front of him,
Remut, the dean, stationed at his side,
They confirm the king's statement, they support his pronouncement,
They bare their heads to swear by oath:
"Until now we did not realize what the king has just explained!"

There is another broken passage in the text in which the defeat of Nabonidus by Cyrus must have been recorded for when
the account is again legible, Cyrus is in control of Babylon:

(Cyrus, the great king), presented his greetings to the Babylonians.
His vizier kept (the troops) away from Ekur,
(He slaughtered cattle), he butchered sheep,
(Incense he placed on) the burners, he provided abundant offerings
      for the Lord of Lords (Marduk),
(He prayed to) the gods, doing obeisance.
The idea came to him to . . .

He made up his mind (to restore Babylon).
(With trowel and) hod he completely repaired the wall of Babylon,
Of his own accord he built (according to the plans of) Nebuchad-
   nezzar II.
. . . fortifications he built on (the wall of Babylon which is called)
   Imgur-Enlil.

(The gods of Babylon), male and female, he returned to their shrines,
(The gods which) had abandoned their (temples) he returned to
   their sanctuaries.
He appeased (their anger), assuaged their wrath,
(Those who were at the) end of endurance he revived,
(Regularly) food was now placed before them. (4)

Fragmentary remains of a few more lines refer to the destruction of Nabonidus' blasphemous works and include encomiums to Cyrus, who has delivered Babylon from these evil times. The same view of the transfer of power from Nabonidus to Cyrus is found in prose form in the so-called "Cyrus Cylinder." Note that, while the theme is the same, in form the document is quite different from the preceding. This is supposed to be a royal inscription of Cyrus while the preceding was a priestly poem. The beginning of the text is missing:

. . . a weakling has been installed to the lordship of his land . . . He made a duplicate of Esagil . . . to the city Ur and the remaining cult centres improper rites . . . daily he would prattle (improper prayers). In a hostile manner he cancelled the offerings . . . everyday without fail he would do evil against his city. All its inhabitants he destroyed with an oppressive yoke. The chief of the gods (Marduk) was enraged by their complaints (and he left) their region. The gods who dwelt amongst them left their sanctuaries, angered that Nabonidus had brought them into Babylon.

But the god Marduk . . . took pity on the people of Sumer and Akkad who had become like corpses, he was appeased and had mercy. Carefully looking through all lands he sought an upright prince after his own heart. Taking him by the hand he pronounced his name: "Cyrus, king of Anshan." He designated him for rule over everything. At his feet he subdued the Qutu and all the Umman-manda. The black-headed people which Marduk had allowed him to conquer he always administered in truth and justice. The god Marduk, the great lord, guardian of his people, looked with joy upon his good works and upright heart. He commanded him to march to his city Babylon. He put him on the road to Babylon and marched all the way at his side like a friend and companion. The extensive troops, which were as immeasurable as water in the river, marched at his side with their weapons packed away. Without battle or strife he brought Cyrus into his city Babylon. Thus did he spare his city hardship. Nabonidus, the king who did not revere Marduk, he handed over to Cyrus. All the people of

Babylon, indeed the entirety of Sumer and Akkad including princes and governors, knelt before Cyrus and kissed his feet. They rejoiced in his sovereignty and their faces were radiant. They appropriately greeted him as the lord with whose help they had been saved from death and who had spared all of them from damage and destruction. They praised his name.

I am Cyrus, king of the universe, great king, strong king, king of Babylon, king of Sumer and Akkad, king of the Four Quarters (of the world), son of Cambyses, great king, king of Anshan, grandson of Cyrus, great king, king of Anshan, offspring of Teispes, great king, king of Anshan, —an ancient royal line; whose reign the gods Marduk and Nabu love, whose sovereignty they desired to make them happy.

When I peacefully entered Babylon and with great rejoicing made the royal palace the administrative headquarters, the god Marduk, the great lord, made the generous hearts of the Babylonians love me and I endeavoured to worship Marduk daily. My extensive army walked about within Babylon peacefully. I did not inflict terrorism in all of Sumer and Akkad. I administered in a peaceful manner within Babylon and all Marduk's cult centres . . . The god Marduk, the great lord, rejoiced in my good works and in a kindly fashion he greeted me, Cyrus, the king, his worshipper, Cambyses, my own son, and all my troops. With a sense of well-being we behaved in a friendly fashion in his presence.

By his exalted command all the kings who sit on daises, of all quarters from the Upper Sea (Mediterranean) to the Lower Sea (Persian Gulf) . . . all the kings of the West who dwell in tents, brought their valuable tribute to me in Babylon and kissed my feet. The district from . . . to Ashur and Susa, Akkad, Eshnunna, Zamban, Meturnu, Der to the border of the land of the Guteans, cult-centres across the Tigris which were founded in ancient times— I returned the gods which dwell in them and made their abode permanent. I gathered all of their people and returned them to their habitations. Also the gods of Sumer and Akkad which Nabonidus, to the anger of the lord of the gods (Marduk), had brought into Babylon, at the command of the god Marduk, the great lord, I safely resettled in their shrines, the abodes where they are glad.

May all the gods which I have restored to their cult-centres daily petition for a long life for me and speak good things about me in the presence of the gods Marduk and Nabu! (5)

> The truth of the matter is that both texts, the Nabonidus Verse Account and the Cyrus Cylinder, were written to justify Cyrus's conquest of Babylonia. The rationalization, or propaganda if one prefers, was done in a very clever way and it appears that Cyrus was wisely magnanimous in his treatment of the conquered state. One gains the same impression from Biblical references to his takeover of Palestine (II Chronicles 36:22f.; Ezra 1; Isaiah 45). In the case of Babylonia Cyrus was fortunate enough to be able to capitalize upon domestic dissatisfaction. As we have seen, a serious rift had developed in Babylonia between the priests and adherents of Marduk and the supporters of the king, Nabonidus, originating in the provincial origin of Nabonidus and his preference for the god Sin over the Babylonian deity, Marduk.
>
> The priestly version is extremely one-sided. There is no doubt that Nabonidus made extravagant claims for Sin (see the first inscription translated in this chapter) and caused him to usurp the supreme position of Marduk in the pantheon. But despite his provincial background, Nabonidus had great respect for some Babylonian traditions. Whenever he undertook to restore a building in Babylonia, he sought out the ancient inscriptions, objects, and foundations of that structure and enthusiastically recorded in his own inscriptions these discoveries. Thus in the first text translated in this chapter he diligently noted finding the inscriptions of kings who ruled fifteen hundred years earlier, Ur-Nammu and Shulgi. Here are a few more typical extracts:

The inscription of Naram-Sin, son of Sargon (of Akkad), I discovered but did not alter. Anointing it with oil and making sacrifices, I deposited it with my inscriptions and thus returned it to its proper place. (6)

Ebabbar, the temple of the god Shamash, which had long ago

become dilapidated and become like a hill of ruins . . . In the reign of Nebuchadnezzar II, a former king, son of Nabopolassar, the sand and mounds of dust which had accumulated on the city and that temple were removed and Nebuchadnezzar discovered the foundation of Ebabbar from the time of Burnaburiash, a former ancient king, but he did not discover the foundation of an older king who preceded Burnaburiash although he looked for it. So he rebuilt Ebabbar on the foundation of Burnaburiash . . . Then Shamash . . . commanded me, Nabonidus . . . to restore Ebabbar . . . the sand which had covered the city and that temple was taken away . . . its foundation appeared and its layout was exposed. I found therein the inscription of Hammurapi, an old king who seven hundred years before Burnaburiash had built Ebabbar and the temple-tower upon an old foundation for Shamash. I was overcome with awe. (7)

He (the god) showed Nabonidus, his reverent servant who looks after his shrines, the foundation of Naram-Sin, son of Sargon (of Akkad). In that year, in a favourable month, on a propitious day, without altering it one finger-length, Nabonidus laid its base on the foundation of Naram-Sin, son of Sargon—the foundation of Ebabbar, temple of Shamash. He discovered the inscription of Naram-Sin and, without altering it, restored it to its proper place. He deposited it with his own inscriptions. He also discovered inside that old foundation a statue of Sargon, father of Naram-Sin. Half of the head was missing, crumbled, so that one could not discern his face. On account of his reverence for the gods and respect for sovereignty, he brought expert craftsmen and had the head of that statue restored and its face reformed. He did not alter its position. He left it inside Ebabbar and presented an oblation for it. (8)

Thus Nabonidus was not the consummate iconoclast portrayed by the Marduk priests. He had great respect for the religious customs and ancient history of Babylonia. It is apparent, therefore, that in their angry reaction to the denigration of Marduk, the Babylonian priests have absurdly overstated their case against Nabonidus. Later, when Cyrus took Babylon, he found it politic to side with the Marduk party and to encourage them to produce such tracts as the Nabonidus Verse Account and the Cyrus Cylinder. Thanks to this biased presentation we shall probably never know the full truth about the character and motives of Nabonidus. Whether the fall of Babylon is largely a result of ill-considered acts on his part or whether it was the next inevitable stage in the expansion of the Persian empire must remain moot. But there is no question that the reputation of Nabonidus has suffered unjustifiably as a result of the fall.

11

"A Barmaid . . . Became King"

Women in Power

The status of women in ancient Mesopotamia was never on a par with that of man although the extent of a woman's rights in the community varied from period to period and even from place to place. An Assyrian woman, for example, was much worse off than her Babylonian counterpart. But regardless of place or time, a Mesopotamian female was regarded as essentially inferior to a male. Thus it was never easy for a woman to gain positions of power—the few who did through the three millennia of Mesopotamian history are dramatic exceptions. In each of these exceptions it may be assumed that special circumstances allied with the unusual character of the woman involved brought the individual in question to power. Unfortunately the nature of our sources does not always allow us to see these two forces at work, but I shall let the reader judge

for himself by proceeding forthwith to the examples of women
in power, and the sources concerning them.

Tradition tells us of a woman in Early Dynastic times who
became queen of Kish. Her name was Ku-Baba and here is the
relevant entry in the Sumerian King List:

In Kish, Ku-Baba, a barmaid, she who made firm the foundation
of Kish, became king and ruled one hundred years. (1)

Several items in this brief note are interesting: This woman
is assigned a dynasty all to herself; she is obviously of low
birth (thus "barmaid"); and she is called "king" by the author
of the list. Just how Ku-Baba came to power is suggested by an
historical omen:

It is the omen of Ku-Baba who seized the sovereignty. (2)

A more fanciful explanation is found in a chronicle: that
those who had respect for the custom of providing fish for the
Marduk cult in Babylon were especially favoured by this god.
The beginning of the entry about Ku-Baba is unfortunately
broken but the remainder is clear:

Ku-Baba gave food and water to the fisherman . . . and he delivered the fish with haste to Esagil. The great lord, Marduk, looked
upon her joyfully and said: "So be it!" He entrusted to Ku-Baba
sovereignty over all lands. (3)

Ku-Baba is the first and only example in Mesopotamian history of a woman gaining sole supreme power. There were, in
the years that followed, outstanding women who exercised
considerable influence at the highest level but, nevertheless,

were never officially recognized as the legitimate rulers. They
always worked through a man, either a husband or a son.
Everyone that we will discuss here was also a foreigner.

At the city-state of Mari on the Upper Euphrates reigned
one Zimri-Lim, a contemporary of Hammurapi (1792–1750
B.C.) of Babylon. Due to the Assyrian capture of Mari, Zimri-
Lim had at one time been forced to flee to Syria where he
found refuge in the court of Aleppo. Here he married a daughter of the king of Aleppo and, in the course of time, when he
drove out the Assyrians he returned to Mari with his Syrian
bride, Shibtu. Shibtu was not content to disappear into the
harem like a normal oriental queen, and through the subsequent turbulent years she took a great interest in affairs of
state and stood staunchly at her husband's side. Zimri-Lim
learned to trust her with important matters and found her
administrative abilities particularly useful when he was absent on military campaigns. Reports from Shibtu to her husband on a variety of administrative matters and problems are
preserved. What is particularly noteworthy is that she was also
entrusted with highly confidential matters. In the following
letter the seizure of "tablets" (i.e. documents) is undertaken
under her supervision. The reason for this action is unknown
but the tone of the letter suggests that the documents were of
an incriminating nature. Perhaps some official or groups of
officials had been abusing their office.

To my lord speak!
The words of Shibtu, your maidservant:
All is well in the palace. My lord wrote to me with the following
instructions: "I am sending Yassur-Adad to you. Send people with
him and wherever he shows them tablets, let them take and put
such tablets in your care until my arrival." I sent with that man
Mukannishum, Shubnalu, and Ut-hirish-tabat, as my lord instructed
me. Yassur-Adad showed to these men, which I sent with him, a
room in the workhouse of . . . Etel-pi-sharrim. They opened the
door of the designated room which was sealed with the seal of
Igmilum of the ministry. They took two baskets of tablets, the

baskets being sealed with the seal of Etel-pi-sharrim. The baskets
with their seals are in my care until my lord arrives. I have sealed
with my seal the door of the room which they opened. (4)

The relationship between Zimri-Lim and Shibtu was not restricted to matters of state. They were, after all, man and wife
and the letters to the campaigning husband are not exclusively administrative in content. Thus in one letter the queen
joyfully announces the birth of twins:

To my lord speak!
The words of Shibtu, your maidservant:
I have given birth to twins—one son and one daughter! Rejoice
my lord! (5)

When we turn to the masculine, militaristic society of Assyria we may, perhaps, not expect to find any examples of
women in power, but there are, in fact, two. Although never
the official head of state, Sammuramat was so influential a
woman that long after the Assyrian empire had disappeared
the legend of her "reign" was remembered. In the work of
the Greek historian, Herodotus, she is called Semiramis. The
legend, insofar as it emphasizes her power, has a factual background as we see in the two documents to be translated. As
to her origin, it is possible that she was a Babylonian princess.
She was married to the Assyrian king Shamshi-Adad V (823–
811 B.C) and was the mother of his successor, Adad-nerari III
(810–783 B.C.). The increase in popularity in Assyrian royal
circles of the worship of the Babylonian god Nabu, which
occurred during the reign of Adad-nerari III, may well be the
responsibility of his mother. In any case, as we see in the following two documents, she did have an unusually privileged
status. The first is an inscription of hers on a stele found at
Ashur. Normally, of course, inscriptions on Assyrian steles are

of kings, or the most important officials. Rarely do they belong to women.

Statue of Sammuramat, palace woman of Shamshi-Adad, king of the universe, king of Assyria; mother of Adad-nerari, king of the universe, king of Assyria; daughter-in-law of Shalmaneser, king of the four quarters. (6)

The second text is found on two statues of the god Nabu discovered at Nimrud. That the dedicatee, an important provincial governor, should dedicate the statue to anyone besides the king is unusual enough, but that it should be a woman is quite atypical for Assyria. This inscription, with the unusually extensive praise of and power attributed to Nabu, also indicates the great importance that Babylonian god has gained in Assyria.

To the god Nabu, heroic, exalted, son of Esagil, splendidly wise, powerful prince, son of Nudimmud, whose command is supreme, master of the arts, trustee of all heaven and underworld, omniscient, of wide understanding, who holds the stylus for the tablet, learned in cunciform, merciful, discerning, who is responsible for abandonment and settlement (of habitations), beloved of the god Enlil, lord of lords, whose strength is unrivalled, without whom there is no counsel in heaven, merciful, compassionate, whose forgiveness is good, dweller of the temple Ezida which is in the city Kalah, the great lord, his lord;

For the life of Adad-nerari, king of Assyria, his lord, and for the life of Sammuramat, the palace woman, his lady, Bel-tarsi-ilima, governor of the city Kalah, and the lands Hamedi, Sirgana, Temeni, Yaluna, and for his own life, the length of his days, the multiplying of his years, the peace of his house and his people, for his preservation from illness, has had made and has presented this statue.

You who come after me, trust in the god Nabu! Do not trust in another god! (7)

Yet another woman of considerable influence in Assyria was Zakutu. She too was a foreigner, an Aramean bride of Sennacherib (704–681 B.C.), and the Aramaic form of her name was Naqia. It was during the latter days of Sennacherib that she began to develop and consolidate her power. The details of the sordid harem plot that led to the murder of Sennacherib, the downfall of his elder sons, and the accession of a younger son Esarhaddon (680–669 B.C.) are unknown. But that Zakutu played a significant role in these events is a reasonable assumption both because Esarhaddon was her own son and because she subsequently assumed considerable power during her offspring's reign. Her control is evident from the following letter which is a report to her rather than the king on an urgent military matter:

To the mother of the king my lord!
The words of your servant Naid-Marduk:
Greetings to the mother of the king my lord! May the gods Ashur, Shamash, and Marduk keep the king my lord in health. May they decree well-being for the mother of the king my lord.
After the Elamites came against us and seized the bridge, I wrote to the mother of the king my lord to report their coming. Now they have ripped up the bridge, tied up the bridge pontoons somewhere, and will not release them. We do not know if they will come again or not. If they should come, I shall report to the mother of the king my lord. Then may my lord order troops for us! (8)

Also from this period of Zakutu's great authority we have two dedicatory inscriptions by her. They are actually found on a clay tablet which provided the pattern for the text which was to be engraved on precious objects.

To the queen, the goddess Ninlil, dweller of the temple Esharra, the great queen, her mistress; Zakutu, the palace woman of Sennacherib, king of the universe, king of Assyria, daughter-in-law of

Sargon, king of the universe, king of Assyria, mother of Esarhaddon, king of Assyria, has had made a . . . of gold in which are set (six precious stones), weighing one and one half minas and five shekels. She installed and dedicated it for the life of Esarhaddon and her own life, for a long life for herself, for the stability of her reign and her well-being.

To the goddess Belit-Ninua, dweller of the temple Emashmash, the great queen, her mistress; Naqia, the palace woman of Sennacherib, king of Assyria, daughter-in-law of Sargon, king of the universe, king of Assyria, has had made a pectoral of red gold in which are set precious stones, weighing three and three quarter minas. She installed and dedicated it for the life of Esarhaddon, king of Assyria, her son, and for her own life, for the stability of her reign and her well-being. (9)

A final example of a woman exercising power in Mesopotamia appears in Babylonia. We have already discussed Nabonidus (555–539 B.C.), the last of the Neo-Babylonian monarchs, in Chapter 10 of this book. Our concern here will be with his mother, Adad-guppi. Like Shibtu, Sammuramat, and Zakutu, Adad-guppi was a foreigner, an Aramean (as was Zakutu). She was a devotee of the god Sin at the city of Harran in Syria. That she played a vital role both in the acquisition of the Babylonian throne by her son and in his subsequent rule is reasonably certain. Here is her inscription found at Harran:

I, Adad-guppi, mother of Nabonidus, king of Babylon, worshipper of the gods Sin, Ningal, Nusku, and Sadarnunna, my gods, whose divinity since my youth I have sought, I who—although in the sixteenth year of Nabopolassar, king of Babylon, Sin, king of the gods, became angry with his city and his temple and ascended to heaven so that the city and the people in it went to ruin—sought out the shrines of Sin, Ningal, Nusku, and Sadarnunna to worship their divinity, I who grasped the hem of the robe of Sin, king of the gods, night and day I constantly seek his great divinity—daily,

without ceasing—I who, so long as I live, am the worshipper of Sin,
Shamash, Ishtar, and Adad who are in heaven and underworld:

Any blessings of mine which they gave me I gave back to them
each day, night, month, and year. I grasped the hem of the robe of
Sin, king of the gods, night and day my eyes were upon him; I
bowed down before him in prayer and humility and thus I prayed:
"May your return to your city take place so that the people, the
black-headed, might worship your great divinity." To appease my
god and my goddess, garments of fine wool, jewels of silver and gold,
new clothing, perfumes, fine oil, I did not bring near to my body,
but wearing torn clothing and going forth meekly I sang their
praises. The glory of my god and goddess was in my heart and I attended to them. Any blessings of mine I did not omit but brought
before them.

From the twentieth year of Ashurbanipal, king of Assyria, when I
was born, until the forty-second year of Ashurbanipal, the third year
of Ashur-etil-ilani, his son, the twenty-first year of Nabopolassar, the
forty-third year of Nebuchadnezzar, the second year of Amil-Marduk,
the fourth year of Neriglissar, for ninety-five years Sin, king of the
gods of heaven and underworld, the shrines of whose great divinity
I sought, who looked joyfully upon me and my good deeds, heard
my prayers and granted my requests. He was appeased. Towards
Ehulhul, the temple of Sin which is in Harran, the dwelling which
pleases him, he was reconciled and had a change of heart. Sin, king
of the gods, looked upon me and appointed Nabonidus my only
son, the issue of my womb, to the sovereignty. He entrusted to him
the sovereignty of Sumer and Akkad and all lands from the border
of Egypt on the Upper Sea to the Lower Sea.

I lifted up my hands and prayed with reverence and piety to Sin,
king of the gods: "Nabonidus, my son, the issue of my womb, beloved of his mother, you have appointed to the sovereignty. You
have pronounced his name. By the command of your great divinity
may the great gods go at his side and may they conquer his foes!
Bring to completion the work on Ehulhul and the perfection of its
rites!" When in my dream his two hands had been laid on, Sin,
king of the gods, said to me: "To your credit is the return of the
gods! I shall entrust to Nabonidus, your son, the shrine at Harran.
He shall rebuild Ehulhul and finish that work. He shall entirely

restore it so that it is better than before. He shall take the hand of Sin, Ningal, Nusku, and Sadarnunna and lead them into Ehulhul." The word of Sin, king of the gods, which he spoke to me I heeded, and I myself saw it fulfilled. Nabonidus, my only son, the issue of my womb, perfected the neglected rites of Sin, Ningal, Nusku, and Sadarnunna. He rebuilt Ehulhul and finished that work. He entirely restored Harran so that it was better than before. He took the hand of Sin, Ningal, Nusku, and Sadarnunna from Babylon his royal city and settled them within Harran in Ehulhul, the dwelling which pleases them, with joy and rejoicing.

What from former times Sin, king of the gods, had not done and had not granted to anybody he did for the love of me who revered his divinity and grasped the hem of his robe: Sin, king of the gods, lifted up my head and established for me a good name in the land. He added to my life long days and years of well-being. He allowed me to live from the time of Ashurbanipal, king of Assyria, until the ninth year of Nabonidus, king of Babylon, my son, the issue of my womb—one hundred and four years of happiness, with the reverence which Sin, king of the gods, instilled in me. The sight of my eyes is clear, my hearing is acute, my hands and feet are sound, my words are well-chosen, food and drink agree with me, I am in good health and my temperament is cheerful. I have seen my great-great-grandchildren, up to my fourth generation of offspring, alive and I am content with my long life.

O Sin, king of the gods, you have looked with favour upon me and lengthened my days. Let me entrust Nabonidus, king of Babylon, my son, to Sin my lord. So long as Nabonidus is alive may he not sin against you. Assign to him the protective genii which you assigned to me and which helped me achieve a long life. Do not ignore his trespasses and sins against your great divinity. But let him revere your great divinity.

With all my heart I have revered and attended to the kings during the twenty-one years of Nabopolassar, king of Babylon, during the forty-three years of Nebuchadnezzar, son of Nabopolassar, and during four years of Neriglissar, king of Babylon, while they exercised sovereignty—altogether sixty-eight years. I put Nabonidus, my son, the issue of my womb, into the service of Nebuchadnezzar, son of Nabopolassar, and Neriglissar, king of Babylon. Day and night he attended to them and always did what was pleasing to them. He established a good reputation for me in their eyes and they took notice of me like one of their own daughters . . . I have made funerary offerings for them and established for them regular offerings of abundant and fragrant incense.

At the end of this inscription appears a description of the death and burial of Adad-guppi, thus proving that the text was not actually completed until after her demise. The passage is badly broken but here is part of it:

In the ninth year of Nabonidus, king of Babylon, she passed away and Nabonidus, king of Babylon, her son, the issue of her womb . . . laid her body to rest. Beautiful robes, bright linen, . . . beautiful stones, . . . precious stones, . . . with fine oil they anointed her corpse and laid it in a secret place. He had fattened rams slaughtered before it. He assembled and brought together the people of Babylon and Borsippa, together with the people dwelling in far regions, kings, princes, and governors, from the border of Egypt on the Upper Sea to the Lower Sea. They instituted the mourning and with grief carried out the weeping . . . seven days and seven nights . . . (10)

The same event is described more laconically in a chronicle entry for the ninth year of Nabonidus:

On the fifth day of the month Nisan the mother of the king died in Dur-karashu which is on the bank of the Euphrates upstream from Sippar. The king's son and his army were in mourning for three days and there was an official mourning period. In the month Sivan there was an official mourning period for the mother of the king in Babylonia. (11)

The figure of Adad-guppi was never forgotten, since she is probably identical with the Nitocris who appears in the Histories of Herodotus. Herodotus, regarding her as more intelligent than Semiramis, devoted considerably more space to a description of her activities. Herodotus assumed as well that she was a queen in full control of Babylonia, which lends further support to the strong impression one has from contemporary sources that she was the guiding hand in Nabonidus's career.

All of the women described in this chapter were exceptional figures in Mesopotamian society. The mere fact that they achieved power despite the low status accorded women in this civilization proves this. But Adad-guppi may have been the exception among exceptions. One has the impression, reinforced by the opinion of Herodotus, that she was more than unusually gifted. The strength of her character, the vast empire which she ruled (indirectly), and her extended life call to mind no less a personage than Queen Victoria.

12

"They Embraced One Another"

Mesopotamian Attitudes Toward Sex

The preoccupation of our present age with sex makes it almost *de rigueur* that, in a book on ancient cultures, one discuss the attitude of the ancients towards it. The inquirer is not disappointed when he looks in ancient Mesopotamian literary remains. There is much erotic material here. But the danger in extracting such passages from their context is that the modern reader is apt to believe that the ancient Mesopotamians, like us, were overly concerned with sex, an attitude which hardly seems justified. The erotic material presented in this chapter is an integral part of larger works which otherwise have nothing to do with sex. For sexual intercourse was simply one of the many facets of life to these ancients. On the other hand they, unlike our Victorian predecessors, had no inhibitions and no feelings of guilt about normal sexual behaviour. A good illustration of this is the Sacred Marriage Texts from

Sumer. In these highly literary religious texts is described most explicitly the annual mating between the king and the high-priestess, an act symbolic of agricultural fertility.

But not all erotic passages appear in a liturgical context. In the Gilgamesh Epic the meeting between the hero, Gilgamesh, and Enkidu is arranged by a prostitute. Enkidu was a wild-man, wandering in the steppe, who had no previous acquaintance with civilization or fellow human-beings. One day a hunter espies him and his report of this strange creature is taken to Gilgamesh, king of Uruk. Gilgamesh commissions a prostitute to go out to the steppe and seduce Enkidu. She succeeds and, having gained a psychological hold over the wild-man, is able to persuade him to go to the city to meet the king.

The hunter went to Gilgamesh,
He took the path and entered Uruk.
He said to Gilgamesh:
"There is a certain young man who has come from the mountains,
He is the strongest in the land, might he possesses,
His might is as great as the constellation of the god Anu.
He is always walking about on the mountains,
With the wild beasts he always eats grass,
His feet always find their way to the watering hole.
I am too frightened to approach him.
He has filled in the pits which I dug,
Ripped out the traps which I laid,
And allowed the wild beasts of the steppe to escape me.
He does not let me work the steppe!"
Gilgamesh said to the hunter:
"Go, hunter, and take a prostitute, a harlot, with you.
When the beasts approach the watering hole,
She will tear off her clothes and display her charms.
When he sees her he will mate with her.
Then the beasts, which grew up with him on the steppe, will become estranged."
The hunter went and took a prostitute, a harlot, with him,
Taking the path they followed the most direct route.

On the third day they reached the destined territory,
The hunter and the prostitute concealed themselves;
One day, two days, they hid at the watering hole.
The beasts came to drink at the watering hole,
The animals came to refresh themselves with water.
Now Enkidu, whose birthplace was the mountain,
Was eating grass with the gazelles,
He was drinking at the watering hole with the beasts,
With the animals he refreshed himself with water.
The harlot saw him, the wild-man,
The savage young man from the interior.
"There he is, harlot, bare your bosom,
Open your vulva that he might possess your charms!
Do not be afraid, receive his ardour.
When he sees you and approaches you,
Take off your clothes that he might lie upon you,
Show him lust, woman's art,
Then the beasts, which grew up with him on the steppe, will be-
    come estranged,
While his passion undulates over you."
The harlot bared her breasts, opened her vulva, and he took pos-
    session of her charms,
She had no fear but received his ardour.
She took off her clothes that he might lie upon her,
She showed him lust, woman's art,
And his passion undulated over her.
For six days and seven nights Enkidu mounted and mated with the
    harlot.
When he was sated with her allure,
He turned towards his beasts;
But when the gazelles saw Enkidu, they darted away,
The beasts of the steppe drew away from his body.
Enkidu was drained, his body felt washed,
His legs stood still, for his beasts had gone.
Enkidu shrank, his stature was not as before.
Then he drew himself up and took in the situation,
Turning around he sat down at the prostitute's feet.
Looking at the prostitute's face,

He listened carefully to what she said.
The prostitute spoke to Enkidu:
"You are becoming as intelligent as a god, Enkidu.
Why do you roam the steppe with animals?
Come, let me take you to fortified Uruk,
To the holy temple, the dwelling of divine Anu and Ishtar,
Where there is Gilgamesh, one perfect in strength,
Where like a wild bull he lords it over the young men."
When she had spoken to him, her words found favour,
He decided to seek a friend and companion.
Enkidu spoke to the prostitute:
"Come, harlot, lead me
To the holy and sacred temple, the dwelling of divine Anu and
    Ishtar,
Where there is Gilgamesh, one perfect in strength,
Where like a wild bull he lords it over the young men." (1)

The prostitute leads Enkidu to Uruk where he meets Gilgamesh. After a wrestling match they become friends and together perform superhuman deeds of valour.
It is while Gilgamesh is tidying up after one of these exploits
that the goddess of love, Ishtar, takes notice of him. It is love
at first sight and Ishtar offers Gilgamesh inducements if he
will but become her lover. Gilgamesh rudely refuses and scorn-
fully reminds Ishtar of the fate of her previous lovers.

Gilgamesh washed his dirty hair, he cleaned his hair bands,
He shook out the hair flowing down his back.
He discarded his dirty clothes and put on clean ones,
He wrapped the garments around him, tying the sash.
Then Gilgamesh donned his crown and
Lady Ishtar cast her eye upon the comeliness of Gilgamesh.
"Come, Gilgamesh, be my lover,
Favour me with your virility.
You will be my husband and I will be your wife,
I will have harnessed for you a chariot of lapis lazuli and gold,

With wheels of gold and horns of amber,
You will hitch up storm demons as great mules.
Enter our temple into the fragrance of cedar,
When you enter our temple,
The noble purification priests will kiss your feet,
Kings, lords, and nobles will bow down before you,
Presenting to you tribute, the produce of mountain and plain.
Your goats will bear triplets, your ewes twins,
Your donkey even while loaded will overtake the mule,
Your horses and chariot will be famous for speed,
Your oxen in harness will have no rival."
Gilgamesh opened his mouth to speak,
He said to Lady Ishtar:
"What must I give to marry you?
Should I give body-oil or garments?
Should I give provisions or food?
I could give you food fit for divinity,
I could give you drink fit for royalty,
(But why should I?)

(You are an oven which cannot melt) ice,
An unfinished door which cannot keep out wind or draught,
A palace which kills warriors,
An elephant which damages its own cover,
Pitch which soils its bearers,
A water-skin which cuts into the side of its bearer,
Limestone which bursts the stone wall,
A siege engine which destroys an enemy fortress,
A shoe which pinches its owner.
Where is your lover who has lasted forever?
Where is your bird who can still ascend?
Come, I will name your lovers!

For Tammuz, your childhood sweetheart,
You decreed regular mourning year after year.
You loved your multi-coloured bird,
And hit him, breaking his wing
So that he sits in the forest crying: "My wing!"
You loved the lion, consummate in strength,

And dug for him seven and seven pits.
You loved the horse, famous in battle,
And decreed for him the whip, goad, and halter,
You decreed that he should run for seven double-hours,
To muddy the water while drinking you decreed for him.
You decreed mourning for his mother, divine Silili.
You loved the shepherd, the herdsman,
Who kept bringing you ash-cakes
And daily slaughtered sacrifices for you;
Him you smote and turned into a wolf
So that his own herders drive him away
And his own dogs bite his heels.
You loved Ishullanu, your father's gardener,
Who kept bringing you baskets of dates
And daily made your table resplendent;
You cast your eye upon him and approached him:
"Ishullanu, let us enjoy your strength!
Pull out your member to meet our vulva!"
But Ishullanu said to you:
"Me! What do you want of me?
Has my mother not baked, have I not eaten,
That I should now be reduced to eating despised and cursed bread?
Do reeds provide protection against the cold?"
When you heard what he said
You struck him and turned him into a frog,
You made him live in misery,

Now it is me you love and you will treat me like them."
When Ishtar heard this,
Ishtar ascended in a rage to heaven.
Ishtar went weeping into the presence of the god Anu, her father,
In the presence of Antu, her mother, her tears flowed:
"My father, Gilgamesh has been cursing me,
Gilgamesh has been relating disgusting stories about me,
Disgusting and damnable things about me."
The god Anu opened his mouth to speak,
He said to Lady Ishtar:
"Listen! Did you not quarrel with king Gilgamesh
And therefore Gilgamesh retold disgusting stories about you,

Disgusting and damnable things about you?"
Ishtar opened her mouth to speak,
She said to the god Anu, her father:
"My father, please give me the Bull of Heaven to kill Gilgamesh . . .
If you do not give me the Bull of Heaven
I will strike (the door and smash the bolt of the Nether World),
I will put those above down below
And I will cause the dead to rise, they will consume the living,
I will make the dead more numerous than the living!" (2)

Ishtar's wrathe calls to mind the words of William Congreve:

"Heav'n has no rage, like love to hatred turn'd,
Nor Hell a fury, like a woman scorn'd."

Ishtar had her way. Anu gave her the Bull of Heaven and the subsequent battle between this terrifying creature and the two friends Gilgamesh and Enkidu is the next major exploit recounted in the epic. The two heroes were successful, slew the bull, and with triumphant scorn Enkidu brandished the bull's thigh in the face of Ishtar, who had been watching from the wall of Uruk, saying:

"If only I could get you like him,
I would do just the same to you!" (3)

In another tale, the epic of Nergal and Ereshkigal, is found the vivid account of how Ereshkigal, goddess of the Nether World, seduced the Upper World deity Nergal who thereby became god of the Nether World. Trouble began when Nergal insulted an emissary of Ereshkigal and he had to descend to the Nether World to apologize. This was a hazardous business and Nergal took care to avoid all the pitfalls except one. While he was in Ereshkigal's presence, the goddess retired briefly to the bathroom and coquettishly gave Nergal a glimpse of her charms. The god, although forewarned that this would happen, fell for the ruse and was seduced by Ereshkigal:

They embraced one another,
Into bed passionately they entered.
The first day, the second day, they slept together, queen Ereshkigal
    and Nergal;
The third day, the fourth day, they slept together, queen Ereshkigal
    and Nergal;
The fifth day, the sixth day, they slept together, queen Ereshkigal
    and Nergal;
When the seventh day arrived,
Since Nergal was not there . . . (4)

Nergal had fled. He had tricked the gatekeeper of the Nether
World and had escaped. Ereshkigal was heartbroken:

Her tears flowed down her cheeks.
"O Nergal, my virile lover!
Before I was sated with his virility he left me.
O Nergal, my virile lover!
Before I was sated with his virility he left me." (5)

But she would not give up easily. She instructed her emissary to go to the chief gods of the Upper World and present
her case in the following manner:

"Since I, your daughter, was a child,
I have not known the frolic of girls
I have not known the romping of youngsters.
That god whom you sent and who mated with me,
Let him sleep with me again,
Send that god to me that he might be my lover,
That he might live with me.
I am sexually impure, I am not without blemish,
I cannot render the judgements of the great gods,
The great gods who reside in the Nether World.

If you do not send that god,
According to the ordinances of the Nether World,
I will cause the dead to rise and they will consume the living,
I will make the dead more numerous than the living!" (6)

As this threat worked for Ishtar, so it worked for Ereshkigal. Nergal attempted to disguise himself in the assembly of the gods but was discovered and conducted back to the Nether World. It appears that Nergal was not overly depressed about his fate for when he again entered Ereshkigal's palace:

He entered her broad courtyard,
He strode up to her and laughed.
He seized her by the hair,
Dragged her from the throne.
He seized her by her tresses,

They embraced one another,
Into bed passionately they entered. (7)

Seven further delirious days followed and thus did Nergal become god of the Nether World.

In Chapter 7 we described how the ancient Mesopotamians found omens in every walk of life. Let us note here that this, of course, included sexual intercourse. In one of the most important ancient treatises on omens, called "If a City is on a Hill," a whole section is devoted to the interpretation of the meaning of various sexual acts. Here is a selection in the order in which the omens appear on the tablet:

If a man has intercourse with a woman, he will quarrel daily.
If a man eats while having intercourse with a woman, . . .
If a man has intercourse with a woman while standing up, . . . that
    man will suddenly have cramps . . .

If a man has intercourse on a roof, the demon "Lord-of-the-Roof" will seize him.

If a man has intercourse in the night and afterwards during a dream he is splattered with his semen, that man will suffer financial loss.

If a man has intercourse with a woman and has a premature emission so that he is splattered with his semen, it is good, that man will have success.

If a man keeps having an emission when approaching an unclean woman, by his virility he will die.

If a man has intercourse with the hindquarters of his equal (male), that man will be foremost among his brothers and colleagues.

If a man keeps saying to his wife: "Present your hindquarters," that man . . . will not have good digestion.

If a man yearns to express his manhood while in prison and thus, like a male cult-prostitute, mating with men becomes his desire, he will experience evil.

If a man habitually has intercourse during the afternoon siesta, that man will have a personal god and be happy.

If a woman mounts a man, that woman will take away the man's virility for one month.

If a man talks with a woman in bed and after rising from the bed he has an erection, that man will be happy and joyful . . . he will always be successful.

If a man is with a woman and in his dreams she keeps looking at his penis, whatever he finds will not be secure in his house.

If a man has intercourse in a wasteland, his wife will bear females.

If a man has intercourse in a field or orchard, his wife will bear males.

If a man has intercourse and then, in the same night, has an emission, that man will experience a serious financial loss.

If a man has an emission during a dream and is splattered with his semen, that man will enjoy good fortune and success.

If a woman keeps grasping a man's penis, it is impure . . .

If a man has intercourse with a cult-prostitute, care will leave him.

If a man has intercourse with a courtier, for one whole year the worry which plagued him will vanish.

If a man has intercourse with his slave, care will seize him. (8)

A problem which concerned the ancient Mesopotamian was the loss of sexual potency. This was of great concern, not only because of the psychological ill-effects, but because of the tremendous importance in Mesopotamian society of begetting one's own children. The physicians and magicians had numerous medications and incantations to correct this debility. Thanks largely to the research of Robert D. Biggs texts describing these are now comprehensible. Here are some examples:

Incantation:
Let the wind blow, let the mountains shake!
Let clouds form, let dew descend!
Let the donkey swell, let him mount the jenny!
Let the buck have an erection, let him keep mounting the she-goat!
Let the buck be tied at the head of my bed,
Let the ram be tied at the foot of my bed.
The one at the head of my bed, get an erection and make love to
    me!
The one at the foot of my bed, get an erection and undulate over
    me!
My vagina is the vagina of a bitch, his penis is the penis of a dog;
As the vagina of a bitch seizes the penis of a dog,
(So may my vagina grasp your penis!)
Let your penis be as long as a sword!
I wait in the midst of a love trap,
May I not miss my prey!
Incantation formula.
(This is an) incantation for potency.

(This is) its ritual:
Into oil put pulverized magnetic iron ore and pulverized iron. Recite the incantation over it seven times. The man rubs his penis, the woman her vagina, with the salve and then he keeps mounting her. (9)

Incantation:
Let the wind blow, let the orchard shake!
Let clouds form, let dew descend!

Let my potency be flowing river water!
Let my penis be a taut harp string
That it will not fall out of her!
Incantation formula.

(This is) its ritual:
Take a harp string and tie three knots in it. Recite the incantation seven times and tie it around his left and right hand. He will again be potent. (10)

Incantation:
I am the daughter of the goddess Ningirsu, who releases (magic spells);
My mother is a releaser, my father a releaser.
I who have come am an expert releaser, I can release!
May the penis of (Fill in Name) son of (Fill in Name) be a stick of hardwood!
May it attack the hindquarters of the woman (Fill in Name)
And never be sated with her charms!
Incantation formula. (11)

Sometimes the problem was not potency, but of persuading the woman to submit to the enamoured male's advances. Thus the magicians were ready to assist with love potions. Here is an example:

Incantation:
The beautiful woman has evoked love.
The goddess Ishtar, who loves apples and pomegranates,
Has brought forth potency.
Stand erect! Give way! Love-stone, prove effective for me! Stand erect!
. . . the goddess Ishtar . . .
She has presided over love.

Incantation:
If a woman casts her eye upon a man's penis.

(This is) its ritual:
Recite the incantation three times either to an apple or a pome-
granate. Give it to the woman and have her suck the juice. Then
that woman will come and you can make love to her.

But if that woman does not come, take flour and throw it into
the river to the god Ea, the king. Take clay from both the opposite
bank of the Tigris and the opposite bank of the Euphrates and
make an image of that woman. Write her name on its left hip. Facing the sun, recite over it the incantation "The Beautiful Woman."
Then bury it at the outer part of the West Gate . . . During the
siesta or during the evening she must walk over it. Recite three times
the incantation "The Beautiful Woman." Then that woman will
come and you can make love to her. (12)

> By this time the reader should be impressed with the absence
> of sexual inhibitions on the part of ancient Mesopotamians.
> Sex was merely part of a normal healthy life. Certain types of
> sexual behaviour were considered anti-social, of course (such as
> adultery), but apart from these few strictures both man and
> god enjoyed love-making to the full. What a contrast this is to
> our modern society, in which much of the material translated
> here, although known to specialists for decades, is presented to
> the general public for the first time!

Glossary for Part One (Egypt)

Abydos—sacred city in the 8th nome (township) of Middle Egypt, associated at an early date with the cult of Osiris.

Alalakh—city in north Syria, modern Tel Atshana; centre of a powerful city-state in the Second Millennium B.C.

Andjety—ancient pastoral deity of the Delta, associated with Osiris.

Anhur—deity of the Abydos nome; a heroic figure who was famed for bringing back to Egypt a savage lioness-goddess.

Anubis—jackal-god of Middle Egypt, associated with the dead.

Amun—originally the township god of the 4th nome of Upper Egypt; later the powerful leader of the pantheon, the "king of the gods."

Avaris—a city in the north-eastern Delta, used by the Hyksos as a residence and strong-point.

Ba-enre Meriamun—the throne name of Merneptah (1224–1215 B.C.).

bai—the projection of the personality, or individuality, of a man, depicted in art as a human-headed bird.

"Big Curl"—lit. "the one with the side-lock," an epithet of the Heliopolitan high-priest.

Busiris—a city in the Delta devoted to the worship of Osiris.

Byblos—Canaanite city on the Phoenician coast, whence the Egyptians imported timber from Lebanon.

Denderah—city of the 6th nome of Upper Egypt, seat of the cult of Hathor, a goddess usually associated with love and music, and sometimes depicted as a lioness.

Double-falcon township—the 5th nome of Upper Egypt.

Ennead—the genealogical cycle of nine deities beginning with the sun-god; sometimes used loosely for the general conclave of deities.

God's-land—a name for any remote country in north or south, which is rich in natural resources.

"Go-incantations"; "Stay-incantations"—two obscure types of magic spells, probably designed respectively to force and restrain the action of the victim.

Great-of-Magic—epithet of the double crown.

Hathor—see "Denderah."

Hatnub—alabaster quarries in Middle Egypt.

Hau-nebu—an ancient name for any remote land or people in the north; early applied to the Aegean islands and their inhabitants.

Hermopolis—important city and metropolis of the 15th nome of Upper Egypt, and seat of the worship of Thoth.

Hordedef—a son of Khufu, second king of the 4th Dynasty; legendary in later times for his wisdom.

Hraihiamun—lit. "Facing Amun"; unidentified town on the west bank at Thebes.

Ibhat—district of the Sudan noted for its building stone.

Imhotpe—architect and physician of King Djoser (c. 2650–2620 B.C.), founder of the 3rd Dynasty.

Indestructables—the circumpolar stars.

Kebebu—a district of Elephantine.

Keftiu—the Egyptian name for a remote land in the north, probably Crete.

khar—a measure of approximately 21 gallons.

Khentiamentiu—lit. "First of Westerners," an epithet of the jackal-god of the dead worshipped at Abydos, and later identified with Osiris.

Khnum—local god of Elephantine at the first cataract, associated with the act of creation.

ku—personification of the life-force of a human being, often depicted in art as a double of its owner.

L.P.H.—a benedictory formula invoking the "life, prosperity and health" of the king or his house.

Letopolis city of the 2nd nome of Lower Egypt, eight miles n-w of modern Cairo.

Memphis—royal residence at the apex of the Delta, traditionally founded by the legendary king Menes, and the centre of administration in the Old Kingdom.

Menkheperre—throne-name of Thutmose III (1490–1436 B.C.).

Menmare—throne name of Sety I (1302–1290 B.C.).

Mentiu—an old name of uncertain origin, used as a general term for the Asiatics of the Negeb and Sinai.

Meretseger—lit. "she who loves silence," a serpent-goddess worshipped in the Theban necropolis.

Mert—goddess of music and singing.

Naharin—name given by the Egyptians to the general area beyond the Euphrates, and often equivalent to Mitanni.

Neferkare—throne name of Pepy II (c. 2294–2200 B.C.).

Neit—an ancient mother-goddess worshipped in the Delta city of Sais.

Nephthys—consort of Seth, and sister of Isis.

Nepry—the god, and personification, of the growing grain.

Onnophris—epithet of Osiris, probably "the perfect existent one."

Pezeshet-towy—lit. "she who apportions the Two Lands," unidentified place in the Memphite township.

Pomegranate-nome—name of the 20th nome of Upper Egypt.

Pwenet—remote tropical country, situated on the coast of East Africa.

ḳrḥt—a little-known serpent associated with kingship.

sed-*festival*—an ancient rite in which the king's coronation was reenacted, and his rule reconfirmed.

serekh—an upright rectangle, representing the facade of the palace, in which the king's Horus name was written.

shawabty—figurine-substitute for the tomb owner, intended to do his compulsory manual labour in the next life.

shōmu—the Egyptian harvest season.

Sobek—the crocodile-god of the Fayum lake.

Sopdu—a falcon(?) god of the eastern townships of the Delta.

Takhsi—the region of Damascus in Syria.

Thebes—city of the 4th nome of Upper Egypt, and, from the triumph of the south over the north in the 21st century B.C., the seat and frequent residence of royalty.

Thinis—city of the 8th nome of Upper Egypt, a little north of Abydos.

Tireless Ones—an epithet of all stars except those which are circumpolar.

Tjemeh—an enclave of foreign tribesmen occupying an ill-defined region west of the Nile in the Libyan desert.

Turah—the limestone quarries east of modern Cairo.

Two Banks—i.e., of the Nile, as a designation of the entirety of the country.

Two Ladies—the goddesses Nekhbit (the vulture) and Edjo (the cobra), the patron deities of Upper and Lower Egypt respectively.

Uraeus—the sacred serpent on the headdress of royalty, associated with the sun-god, and often identified as his fierce "Eye."

Usermare Setepnre—throne name of Ramesses II (1290–1224).

Wag-feast—a festival associated with Osiris on the 18th day of the first calendar month, when offerings were made to the dead.

Wepwawet—lit. "trail-blazer," a jackal god connected with the desert and the necropolis, whose standard is often depicted in festal processions leading the king.

Glossary for Part Two (Mesopotamia)

Adad—The god of storm and, together with Shamash, god of divination.

Akkad—The name of the capital founded by Sargon (location unknown) and also of the northern part of the Babylonian plain. The southern part is called Sumer.

Anu—Supreme god in the Sumerian pantheon and tutelary deity of Uruk.

Ashur—This is the name of both the city and its god. In the imperial period the city Ashur, although not always the political capital, was still the religious and cultural centre of Assyria.

Elam—An ancient civilization on the eastern border of Sumer/Babylonia. The capital was Susa.

Enlil—Second only to Anu in the Sumerian pantheon. In Sumerian mythology Enlil actually appears more important than Anu. In later periods he was equated to Marduk and Ashur. His spouse was Ninlil and his city Nippur.

Esagil—Marduk's temple at Babylon.

Ishtar—The most important goddess in ancient Mesopotamia and in general one of the most important deities. She was responsible for love and war. Officially she was the spouse of Anu.

Marduk—Supreme god of the Babylonian pantheon.

Mari—A city-state on the Middle Euphrates where a large corpus of Akkadian documents from the Old Babylonian period was discovered.

Nabu—Son of Marduk, tutelary god of Borsippa, and god of scribes.

Ninlil—Consort of Enlil. When Enlil was equated with Ashur, she was his spouse.

Shamash—The sun god, tutelary god of Sippar, god of justice, and, together with Adad, the god of divination.

Sumer—In addition to being a term for that ancient civilization this word can refer to the southern part of the Babylonian plain. See Akkad.

Bibliography

GENERAL

Bottéro, J., et al., *The Near East: The Early Civilizations* (New York: Delacorte Press, 1967).
Cambridge Ancient History, Vols. 1–4, Cambridge: Cambridge University Press.
Hallo, W. W., and Simpson, W. K., *The Ancient Near East: A History* (New York: Harcourt Brace Jovanovich, Inc., 1971).

EGYPT

Gardiner, A., *Egypt of the Pharaohs* (Oxford Press, 1961).
Kees, H., *Ancient Egypt, A Cultural Topography* (London: Faber & Faber, 1961).

Wilson, J., *The Culture of Ancient Egypt* (New York: Phoenix Books, 1957).

MESOPOTAMIA

Oppenheim, A. L., *Ancient Mesopotamia* (Chicago and London: University of Chicago Press, 1964).
Roux, G., *Ancient Iraq* (London: George Allen and Unwin, 1964).
Saggs, H. W. F., *The Greatness That Was Babylon* (London: Sidgwick and Jackson, 1962).

FURTHER READINGS FOR INDIVIDUAL CHAPTERS

Chapter 1:

H. Frankfort, *Kingship and the Gods* (Chicago: University of Chicago Press, 1948).
G. Steindorff, K. C. Seele, *When Egypt Ruled the East* (New York: Phoenix Books, 1963).

Chapter 2:

J. Wilson, *The Culture of Ancient Egypt* (New York: Phoenix Books, 1957).

Chapter 3:

W. B. Emery, *Egypt in Nubia* (London: Hutchinson, 1965).
W. S. Smith, *Interconnections in the Ancient Near East* (New Haven: Yale University Press, 1965).

Chapter 4:

J. H. Breasted, *Ancient Records of Egypt*, vol. I (Chicago: University of Chicago Press, 1906).

Chapters 5 and 6:

A. Erman (W. K. Simpson, ed.), *The Ancient Egyptians: a Source Book of Their Writings* (New York: Harper Torchbooks, 1966).
W. K. Simpson (ed.), *The Literature of the Ancient Egyptians* (New Haven: Yale University Press, 1972).

Chapter 7:

Finkelstein, J. J., "Mesopotamian Historiography" in *Proceedings of the American Philosophical Society*, 107 (1963), pp. 461–472.
Jacobsen, T., "Mesopotamia" in *The Intellectual Adventure of Ancient Man*, H. Frankfort, et al. (Chicago: University of Chicago Press, 1946).
Kramer, S. N., "Sumerian Historiography" in *Israel Exploration Journal*, 3 (1953), pp. 217–232.
Speiser, E. A., "Ancient Mesopotamia" in *The Idea of History in the Ancient Near East*, ed. R. C. Dentan (New Haven: Yale University Press, 1955).

Chapter 8:

Olmstead, A. T., *History of Assyria* (Chicago and London: University of Chicago Press, 1923).
Smith, S., *Early History of Assyria to 1000 B.C.* (London: Chatto and Windus, 1928).

Chapter 9:

Brinkman, J. A., "Merodach-baladan II" in *Studies Presented to A. Leo Oppenheim*, ed. R. D. Biggs and J. A. Brinkman (Chicago: The Oriental Institute of the University of Chicago, 1964), pp. 6–53.

Chapter 10:

Dougherty, R. P., *Nabonidus and Belshazzar*, Yale Oriental Series, Researches 14 (New Haven: Yale University Press, 1929).

Chapter 11:

Artzi, P., and Malamat, A., "The Correspondence of Šibtu, Queen of Mari in ARM X" in *Orientalia,* n.s. 40 (1971), pp. 75–89.
Gordon, C. H., "The Status of Woman Reflected in the Nuzi Texts" in *Zeitschrift für Assyriologie,* 43 (1936), pp. 146–169.

Chapter 12:

Kramer, S. N., *The Sacred Marriage Rite* (Bloomington, Indiana: University Press, 1969).
Lambert, W. G., "Divine Love Lyrics from Babylon" in *Journal of Semitic Studies,* 4 (1959), pp. 1–15.

Sources of Texts Translated

ABBREVIATIONS

ABC Grayson, A. K., *Assyrian and Babylonian Chronicles, Texts from Cuneiform Sources,* 5 (Glückstadt and New York: J. J. Augustin, 1973).

ABL Harper, R. F., *Assyrian and Babylonian Letters* (London and Chicago: University of Chicago Press, 1892–1914).

AfO *Archiv für Orientforschung.*

AKA Budge, E. A. W. and King, L. W., *Annals of the Kings of Assyria* (London: British Museum, 1902).

ANET Pritchard, J. B. (ed.), *Ancient Near Eastern Texts Relating to the Old Testament,* 3rd edition (Princeton: Princeton University Press, 1969).

AnSt *Anatolian Studies*

ARAB   *Ancient Records of Assyria and Babylonia* (Chicago: University of Chicago Press, 1926–7).

ARI   Grayson, A. K., *Assyrian Royal Inscriptions* 1 (Wiesbaden: Otto Harrassowitz, 1972).

ARM   *Archives Royales de Mari.*

ASAE   *Annales du Service des Antiquités de l'Egypte.*

BAL   Borger, R., *Babylonisch-Assyrische Lesestücke* (Rome: Pontificium Institutum Biblicum, 1963).

BBSt   King, L. W., *Babylonian Boundary-Stones and Memorial-Tablets in the British Museum* (London: British Museum, 1912).

BHT   Smith, S., *Babylonian Historical Texts Relating to the Capture and Downfall of Babylon* (London: Methuen and Co., Inc., 1924).

BIFAO   *Bulletin de l'Institut Français d'Archéologie Orientale.*

Biggs, ŠÀ.ZI.GA   Biggs, R. D., *ŠÀ.ZI.GA, Ancient Mesopotamian Potency Incantations, Texts from Cuneiform Sources, 2* (Glückstadt and New York: J. J. Augustin, 1967).

BiOr   *Bibliotheca Orientalis.*

Borger, Asarh.   Borger, R., *Die Inschriften Asarhaddons Königs von Assyrien,* AfO Beiheft 9 (Graz: Ernst Weidner, 1956).

CAH   *Cambridge Ancient History.*

CT   *Coffin Texts.*

EA   Knudtzon, J. A., *Die El-Amarna-Tafeln,* VAB 2 (Leipzig, 1907–1915).

FIFAO   *Fouilles de l'Institut Français d'Archéologie Orientale*

IAK   Ebeling, E., Meissner, B., Weidner, E., *Die Inschriften der Altassyrischen Könige,* Altorientalische Bibliothek 1 (Leipzig: Quelle und Meyer, 1926).

JCS   *Journal of Cuneiform Studies.*

JEA   *Journal of Egyptian Archaeology.*

JNES   *Journal of Near Eastern Studies.*

OIP   *Oriental Institute Publications.*

Parpola, *Letters*   Parpola, S., *Letters from Assyrian Scholars to the Kings Esarhaddon and Assurbanipal, Part I: Texts, Alter Orient und Altes Testament* 5/1 (Neukirchen-Vluyn: Verlag Butzon und Bercker Kevelaer, 1970).

PT   *Pyramid Texts.*

R   Rawlinson, H. C., et al., *The Cuneiform Inscriptions of Western Asia* 5 vols. (London: British Museum, 1861–1884).

RA   *Revue d'Assyriologie et d'Archéologie Orientale.*

REA   *Revue d'Egypte Ancienne.*

RT   *Recueil de Travaux relatifs à la Philologie et à l'Archéologie Egyptienne et Assyrienne.*

SAK   Thureau-Dangin, F., *Die Sumerischen und Akkadischen Königsinschriften*, VAB 1 (Leipzig, 1907, J. C. Hinrichs).

TCL   *Textes Cunéiformes du Louvre.*

Thompson, Gilg.   Thompson, R. C., *The Epic of Gilgamish* (Oxford: Clarendon Press, 1930).

VAB   *Vorderasiatische Bibliothek.*

Waterman, *Royal Correspondence*   Waterman, L., *Royal Correspondence of the Assyrian Empire* (Ann Arbor: University of Michigan Press, 1930–36).

WO   *Die Welt des Orients.*

ZA   *Zeitschrift für Assyriologie.*

ZÄS   *Zeitschrift für Ägyptische Sprache.*

ZZB   Edzard, D. O., *Die Zweite Zwischenzeit Babyloniens* (Wiesbaden: Otto Harrassowitz, 1957).

CHAPTER 1

1. PT spell 303: K. Sethe, *Die altägyptische Pyramidentexte* (Leipzig: J. C. Hinrichs, 1908–1922), I, 239ff.
2. Theban ostracon: A. H. Gardiner, *JEA* 5 (1918), 190.
3. Biography of Amenemheb: K. Sethe, *Urkunden der 18. Dynastie* (Berlin: Akademie Verlag, 1961), 895f.
4. Sallier I, 8, 7ff: Sir A. H. Gardiner, *Late Egyptian Miscellanies* (Brussels: Fondation Reine Elisabeth, 1937), 86f.
5. Biographical text of Nebamun: N. de G. Davies, A. H. Gardiner, *The Tombs of Two Officials of Tuthmosis IV* (London: Egypt Exploration Society, 1923), pl. 26.
6. Induction of Nebwennef: K. Sethe, *ZÄS* 67 (1931), pl. 1–2.
7. Admonition of the Vizier: K. Sethe, *Urkunden der 18. Dynastie* (Berlin: Akademie Verlag, 1961), 1087ff.

8. Reception of Sinuhe: A. M. Blackman, *Middle Egyptian Stories* (Brussels: Fondation Reine Elisabeth, 1932), 36ff.
9. Revue of Tribute: W. Helck, *Urkunden der 18. Dynastie* (Berlin: Akademie Verlag, 1961), 1345f.
10. Decree of Pepy II: H. Goedicke, *Königliche Dokumente aus dem alten Reich* (Wiesbaden: Otto, Harrassowitz, 1967), 87ff.
11. The Instruction for Merikare: A. Volten, *Zwei altägyptische politische Schriften* (Copenhagen: Einar Munksgaard, 1945), 3ff.

CHAPTER 2

1. Merikare: Volten, *ibid.*, 47f.
2. Stela of Senwosret III: J. M. A. Janssen, *JNES* 12 (1953), pl. 65.
3. Semneh stela of a viceroy of Amenophis II: W. Helck, *JNES* 14 (1955), pl. 2.
4. Anastasi VI, 50–61: Gardiner, *Late Egyptian Miscellanies* (Brussels: Fondation Reine Elisabeth, 1937), 76f.
5. The Prophecy of Neferty: W. Helck, *Die Prophezichung des Nfr.tj* (Wiesbaden: Otto Harrassowitz, 1970), 16ff.
6. Biography of Pepy-nakht: K. Sethe, *Urkunden des alten Reichs* (Leipzig: J. C. Hinrichs, 1903), 131ff.
7. Merikare: Volten, *op. cit.*, 41ff.
8. Yebya[e]: H. O. Lange, H. Schäfer, *Grab- und Denksteine des Mittleren Reichs* (Cairo: Institut français, 1902–25), no. 20086.
9. The Treasurer Sobekhotpe: Sir A. II. Gardiner, *et al., The Inscriptions of Sinai* (London: Oxford University Press, 1952), pl. 85, no. 405.
10. Amenemhet: J. Couyat, P. Montet, *Les Inscriptions Hiéroglyphiques et Hiératiques du Ouâdi Hammamat* (Cairo: Institut français, 1912–13), pl. 13, no. 43.
11. Hetcpy: *ibid.*, pl. 5, no. 17.
12. Ptah-wer: Gardiner, *Sinai*, pl. 18, no. 54.
13. Sinuhe: B 70ff.
14. First Kamose Stela: A. H. Gardiner, *JEA* 3 (1916), 95ff, pl. 12–13.
15. Second Kamose Stela: L. Habachi, *ASAE* 53 (1955), 195ff.

16. Tombos Stela of Thutmose I: Sethe, *Urkunden der 18. Dynastie* (Berlin: Akademie Verlag, 1961), 82ff.
17. Gebel Barkal Stela: Helck, *Urkunden der 18. Dynastie* (Berlin: Akademie Verlag, 1957), 1277ff.
18. Minmose: *ibid.*, 1448.
19. Amenhotpe III's mortuary endowment: *ibid.*, 1649.
20. Letter of Bakenamun: Bologna 1086.
21. Testament of Si-Bast: Helck, *Urkunden der 18. Dynastie* (Berlin: Akademie Verlag, 1957), 1369.

CHAPTER 3

1. Ipuwer's lament: A. H. Gardiner, *The Admonitions of an Egyptian Sage* (Leipzig, J. C. Hinrichs, 1909).
2. Strike papyrus: Sir A. H. Gardiner, *Ramesside Administrative Documents* (Oxford: Oxford University Press, 1948), 49ff.
3. Ramesses III's address: W. Erichsen, *Papyrus Harris* I (Brussels: Fondation Reine Elisabeth, 1933), p. 91.

CHAPTER 4

(A) THE DECEASED REQUESTS:

1. Sethe, *Urkunden des Alten Reichs* (Leipzig: J. C. Hinrichs, 1903), 120f.
2. *Idem, Urkunden der 18. Dynastie* (Leipzig: J. C. Hinrichs, 1903), 1032.
3. O. Koefoed-Peterson, *Publications de la Glyptothèque Ny Carlsberg no. 1: les stèles égyptiennes* (Copenhagen, Foudation Ny Carlsberg, 1948), no. 9.
4. Lange, Schäfer, *op. cit.*, no. 20003.
5. D. Dunham, *Semna-Kummeh* (Boston: Museum of Fine Art, 1960), pl. 91D.

(B) THE DECEASED THREATENS:

1. Sethe, *Urkunden des Alten Reichs* (Leipzig: J. C. Hinrichs, 1903), 23.

2. *Ibid.*, 150.
3. R. Anthes, *Die Felseninschriften von Hatnub* (Leipzig: J. C. Hinrichs, 1928), no. 49.

(C) THE DECEASED NARRATES:

1. Sethe, *Urkunden des Alten Reichs* (Leipzig, 1903), 98ff.

(D) THE DECEASED BOASTS:

1. Dunham, *Naga-ed-dêr Stelae* (London, Oxford University Press, 1937), no. 78.
2. Sir W. M. F. Petrie, *Dendereh* (London, 1900), pl. 11.
3. Anthes, *op. cit.*, no. 22.
4. J. Vandier, *Mo'alla. La Tombe d'Ankhtifi et la Tombe de Sébekhotep* (Cairo: Institut français, 1950), Insc. 2.
5. *Ibid.*, Insc. 6.

CHAPTER 5

1. The Tale of the Shipwrecked Sailor: De Buck, *Egyptian Readingbook* (Leiden: E. J. Brill, 1948), 100ff.
2. The Tale of Apophis and Seqnenre: Gardiner, *Late Egyptian Stories* (Brussels: Fondation Reine Elisabeth, 1931), 85ff.
3. The Story of the Doomed Prince: *ibid.*, 1ff.

CHAPTER 6

1. The Tale of Two Brothers: *ibid.*, 9ff.
2. Book of the Heavenly Cow: De Buck, *Egyptian Readingbook* (Leiden: E. J. Brill, 1948), 123ff.
3. The Trial of Horus and Seth: Gardiner, *Late Egyptian Stories* (Brussels: Fondation Reine Elisabeth, 1931), 37ff.

CHAPTER 7

1. Grayson, ABC Chron. 1 iii 13–18.
2. Luckenbill, OIP 2, pp. 88f.:44–48. Cf. Luckenbill, ARAB 2, §§ 344–352.
3. Harper, ABL 46 r. 10. Cf. Parpola, Letters 1, no. 298.
4. Nougayrol, RA 40 (1945–6), p. 91:38–40.
5. Thureau-Dangin, RA 22 (1925), p. 23.
6. Goetze, JCS 1 (1947), p. 260.
7. Grayson and Lambert, JCS 18 (1964), pp. 12–16.
8. Gurney, AnSt 5 (1955), pp. 93–113 and 6 (1956), pp. 163f. and Finkelstein, JCS 11 (1957), pp. 83–88.

CHAPTER 8

1. Thureau-Dangin, *SAK* p. 154, i 36–ii 20. Cf. Gadd, *Dynasty of Agade*-CAH I, Chapter 19, pp. 6f.; Edzard, in J. Bottéro, et al., *The Near East* (New York: Delacorte Press, 1967), pp. 83f.
2. Hirsch, AfO 20 (1963), p. 36 iii/iv 7–12. Cf. *ibid.* p. 3.
3. Hirsch, AfO 20 (1963), p. 38 v 14–28 and vi 17–35. Cf. ibid. p. 3; Gadd, *Dynasty of Agade* p. 10; Edzard, *The Near East* p. 106.
4. Grayson, ABC Chron. 20 A 4–6 and Corrigenda.
5. Meissner, IAK p. 24 iv 5–18. Cf. Grayson, ARI 1, XXXIX, 1; Malamat, in *Studies in Honor of B. Landsberger,* ed. H. G. Güterbock and T. Jacobsen (Chicago: University of Chicago Press, 1965), pp. 370–372.
6. Weidner, IAK pp. 116–118 ii 16–40. Cf. Grayson, ARI 1, LXXVII, 1.
7. Weidner, IAK pp. 114–116 i 39–ii 13. Cf. Grayson, ARI 1, LXXVII, 1.
8. King, AKA pp. 334–341 ii 103–118 and pp. 343f. ii 125–128. Cf. Luckenbill, ARAB 1, §§ 436–484.
9. King, AKA pp. 341–343 ii 118–125 and cf. *ibid.* pp. 237f.: 36–41. Cf. Luckenbill, ARAB 1, § 466.
10. Thureau-Dangin, TCL 3:51–63. Cf. Luckenbill, ARAB 1, §§ 148f.

11. Grayson, AfO 20 (1963), pp. 88–94:11–16, 60–63, 66–68, 85–91, 93–101 and cf. Borger, BAL pp. 76–78. Cf. Luckenbill, ARAB 1, §§ 232–254.
12. Grayson, ABC Chron. 5:5–13.

CHAPTER 9

1. Grayson, ABC Chron. 1 i 1–5.
2. Saggs, Iraq 17 (1955), pp. 23–26 and pl. IV.
3. Saggs, Iraq 25 (1963), pp. 71–73 and pl. XI.
4. Grayson, ABC Chron. 1 ii 1–5.
5. Borger, BAL pp. 62f. i 20–35. Cf. Luckenbill, ARAB 2, §§ 232–254.
6. Borger, BAL pp. 70f. iii 50–70. Cf. Luckenbill, ARAB 2, §§ 232–254.
7. Luckenbill, OIP 2, pp. 83f.:43–54. Cf. Luckenbill, ARAB 2, §§ 330–343.
8. Borger, Asarh. pp. 15–20 and cf. Borger, BiOr 21 (1964), pp. 143–145. Cf. Luckenbill, ARAB 2, §§ 639–646.
9. Grayson, ABC Chron. 16:9–27.
10. Oppenheim, Iraq 17 (1955), pp. 87f.
11. Oppenheim, Iraq 17 (1955), p. 89.
12. Grayson, ABC Chron. 3:1–45.

CHAPTER 10

1. Langdon, VAB 4, Nab. no. 5.
2. Dynastic Prophecy ii 11–16 to be published by Grayson.
3. Grayson, ABC Chron. 7 ii 5–12.
4. Smith, BHT no. 4 and Landsberger and Bauer, ZA 37 (1927), pp. 88–95. Cf. Oppenheim, ANET³ pp. 312–315.
5. Weissbach, VAB 3, pp. 2–9. Cf. Oppenheim, ANET³ pp. 315f.
6. Langdon, VAB 4, Nab. no. 1 iii 8–10.
7. Langdon, VAB 4, Nab. no. 3 i 33–ii 27.
8. Lambert, AfO 22 (1968–69), pp. 1–8:21–36.

CHAPTER 11

1. T. Jacobsen, The Sumerian King List (Chicago: University of Chicago Press, 1939), p. 104 v 36–39.
2. Nougayrol, RA 38 (1941), p. 84:28f. and cf. RA 40 (1945–6), p. 90.
3. Grayson, ABC Chron. 19:43–45.
4. Dossin, ARM 10, no. 12. Cf. W. H. Ph. Römer, *Frauenbriefe über Religion, Politik, und Privatleben in Mari* (Neukirchen-Vluyn: Verlag Butzon und Bercker Kevelaer, 1971), pp. 83–85.
5. Dossin, ARM 10, no. 26. Cf. Römer, *Frauenbriefe* p. 60.
6. W. Andrae, *Die Stelenreihen in Assur* (Leipzig: J. C. Hinrichs, 1913), no. 5. Cf. Luckenbill, ARAB 1, §§ 730–1.
7. Norris, I R 35, no. 2. Cf. Luckenbill, ARAB 1, § 744–5.
8. Harper, ABL no. 917:1–15. Cf. M. Dietrich, *Die Aramäer Südbabyloniens in der Sargonidenzeit* (Neukirchen-Vluyn: Verlag Butzon und Bercker Kevelaer, 1970), pp. 144f.
9. C. H. W. Johns, *Assyrian Deeds and Documents* (Deighton, Bell and Co. Ltd. Cambridge, 1898–1923), no. 645 and cf. J. Kohler and E. Ungnad, *Assyrische Rechtsurkunden* (Leipzig: Eduard Pfeiffer, 1913), no. 14.
10. Gadd, AnSt 8 (1958), pp. 46–56. Cf. Oppenheim, ANET³ pp. 560–562.
11. Grayson, ABC Chron. 7 ii 13–15.

CHAPTER 12

1. Thompson, Gilg. I iii 26–iv 46. Cf. Speiser, ANET³ pp. 74f.
2. Thompson, Gilg. VI 1–100. Cf. Speiser, ANET³ pp. 83f.
3. Thompson, Gilg. VI 162–163. Cf. Speiser, ANET³ p. 85.
4. Gurney, AnSt 10 (1960), p. 118 iv 9'–15'. Cf. Grayson, ANET³ p. 510.
5. Gurney, AnSt 10 (1960), p. 120 iv 52'–56'. Cf. Grayson, ANET³ pp. 510f.
6. Gurney, AnSt 10 (1960), p. 122 v 2'–12'. Cf. Grayson, ANET³ p. 511.

7. Gurney, AnSt 10 (1960), p. 126 vi 29–36. Cf. Grayson, ANET [3] p. 512.
8. C. J. Gadd, *Cuneiform Texts from Babylonian Tablets, etc. in the British Museum* 39 (London: British Museum, 1926), 44f.
9. Biggs, ŠÀ.ZI.GA no. 14.
10. Biggs, ŠÀ.ZI.GA no. 15.
11. Biggs, ŠÀ.ZI.GA no. 22.
12. Biggs, ŠÀ.ZI.GA p. 70.

Index